LEARNING FROM THE APOSTLES

lessons for today from their lives and witness

Amos D. Millard

GOSPEL PUBLISHING HOUSE
Springfield Missouri

02-0537

LEARNING FROM THE APOSTLES

1445 Boonville Avenue
Springfield, Missouri 65802

This is a Workers Training Division textbook. Credit for its study will be issued under Classification 1 National Sunday School Department Assemblies of God

Printed in the United States of America

Introduction

We are living in a day of introspection and reexamination. A new generation is examining old foundations with an attitude of skepticism, and the words "change" and "relevant" are common in their conversations.

In a number of respects this age is similar to the one which ushered in the Christian church almost two thousand years ago. Samuel Angus described that era as one of change and upheaval. "Men were driven from their old moorings and had not yet become accustomed to the new order. The average man was perplexed by the rapid march of history. In the social confusion and the fall of long-established 'system' there was much to unsettle the firmest faith. Such transition periods are always fraught with difficulties and danger."

These words could not have been precipitated by any comparison of that age with the "jet age." They were written in 1914.

Within many quarters of the Christian church this process of change has been radical. Not only have the Church's traditional beliefs and teachings been challenged, but so has its authority as an institution. These are changes that Biblically versed people should fully expect. They are among the signs of our Lord's return.

It is timely that we in the Pentecostal Movement should study the Biblical foundations of our existence. Our Movement is relatively young as far as modern church movements go. Yet it is rooted in the same soil of faith and truth as the Early Church. What the modern Pentecostal Movement demonstrates more than anything else is that the principles upon which the Apostolic Church was founded are still valid and are still operative.

It is an inescapable conclusion that the Early Church was a "Pentecostal" church and that there was divine intent that this pattern should be the normative pattern for the Church throughout its history. The experience of the Church at Pentecost was not for the 120 and that generation only, but it was "to your children, and to all that are afar off, even as many as the Lord our God shall call" (Acts 2:39).

Thus our modern Pentecostal Movement was founded through the leadership of the Holy Spirit Himself. Our mission in this critical hour of the world's history is not to be just another denomination. It is to be a witness to the reality and the power of the gospel. Within seventy years of this present-day outpouring of the Spirit, we have witnessed a growth and a penetration of the Movement unto the ends of the earth. We are witnessing a new openness to the Holy Spirit among many, if not all, of the major church bodies; and it remains to be seen what God will do through them as they yield to the Spirit's leadership.

The vitality and effectiveness of our Movement will be assured by the continual moving of the Spirit and by our fidelity to the Word of God. It is in respect to the second that the task of *teaching* is summoned. The principles of teaching God's Word are set forth in both Testaments. The Word starts from the *heart* of the teacher. God told Israel, "And these words, which I command thee this day, shall be in thine *heart:* and thou shalt *teach* them diligently unto thy children, and shalt talk of them when thou sittest in thine house, and when thou walkest by the way, and when thou liest down, and when thou risest up" (Deuteronomy 6:6, 7).

The New Testament concern is no less involved with the spiritual life and character of the teacher. In his farewell letter Paul said, "And the things that thou hast heard of me among many witnesses, the same commit thou to *faithful* men, who shall be able to *teach* others also" (2 Timothy 2:2). Paul's concern about the character of the teacher comes first: He is to be *faithful;* and this is a term that comprehends much more than regularity, but loyalty to Jesus and integrity of heart and life. Then ability comes second: "able to teach others also."

The need for the Church's ministry in the power of the Spirit to the world has never been more urgent. Human problems, while basically the same throughout history, are intensified today by the sheer weight of the world's burgeoning population. But there is yet another factor which intensifies the urgency of this hour: it is the *lateness* of the hour. The signs that Jesus and the apostles gave us point unmistakably to the end time. We are faced with that same sense of urgency that overtook our Lord toward the close of His earthly ministry when He said, "I must work the works of him that sent me, while it is day: the night cometh, when no man can work" (John 9:4).

Contents

1 : The Church's Mission

It happened near the ancient city of Caesarea Philippi. The setting was one of grandeur. Nestled almost 1,200 feet above sea level in a valley, the city was framed in the "trough" of the Lebanon Mountain range. To the east towered snow-mantled Mt. Hermon. To the west was the high Lebanon range, bordering the sea. Behind the city were two geological features, both of which were to provide the symbols for what Jesus was about to say to His disciples. One was an abrupt rock wall, solid and stalwart. The other was a huge cavern in the side of the mountain, out of which burst forth one of the sources of the Jordan River.

To the ancients the cave was the Sanctuary of Pan, a heathen sanctuary and a vestibule to hades, the underworld. Nearby was a gleaming white marble temple, dedicated to the Roman Emperor, Augustus Caesar. These two great heathen forces held captive men's souls in prisons of heathen darkness. Opposed to them, the church of Jesus Christ would stand, founded upon Christ Himself. In the days to follow, Christianity would come into conflict with heathen forces in varied forms. It is at this point and in this setting that Jesus' response to Peter's confession deserves careful study. Jesus not only defined the Church's mission and message, but He described its reception by the world. It is, in short, a picture of battle and warfare.

Peter's words evoked from Jesus both a blessing and a prophecy: "And I say also unto thee, That thou art Peter, and upon this rock I will build my church; and the gates of hell shall not prevail against it" (Matthew 16:18). In this statement are two fundamental declarations about the future of the Church: (1) The Church was to be founded on a solid foundation. It was the foundation of Christ Himself, who was revealed to them—and us—as the Son of the Living God; (2) The Church's mission in the world would be a conflict with heathen forces, which Jesus described as the "gates of hell" (hades).

It should be noted when groups or individuals tamper with the foundational truth of the deity of Christ, they tamper with the foundation of faith upon which the Church is chartered. In so doing, they forfeit the promise of Christ to Peter and to every believer who receives Christ as the Son of God. It was with the advent of "modern criticism" before the turn of the last century that the deity of Christ, His virgin birth, His miraculous life, and His resurrection began to be denied on a popular scale. Today the churches which heeded such denials are beleaguered by a loss of spiritual power, authority, and public respect.

Thus it was at the entrance to this beautiful valley high in the Lebanon Mountains that Jesus predicted the conflict between His Church and the forces of hell. "I will build my church; and the gates of hell shall not prevail against it" (Matthew 16:18). To the north of where the disciples stood was another vast heathen temple complex, known today as Balbek. It was the Roman Empire's last all-out attempt to revive and to popularize the Graeco-Roman religious system. Still farther north, at the northern exit of this valley from where the Orontes River emptied into the sea, stood a third heathen center,

Antioch of Syria. It was so degraded by foul practices that even the ancient Roman satirist, Juvenal, could find no greater barb of sarcasm against Rome than to suggest that the "Orontes had flowed into the Tiger," inundating Rome with the depravity of Antioch. Yet Antioch became the first missionary center outside of Palestine from which the gospel of Christ was disseminated throughout the Mediterranean world. It was here the name "Christian" was given to the "followers of the Way" (i.e., Christ).

The Church's mission would be at the "gates of hell." Herein was a figure familiar to ancients. The gates of ancient cities were the most vulnerable point of attack in warfare. An invading army would storm the gates to break them down and gain access into the city. Thus Jesus implied that His Church would be on the offensive, not the defensive. The Church would take missionary initiative by *going* to the world. Lillian Trasher's *going* to Egypt and David Wilkerson's *going* to the haunts of Harlem with the gospel illustrate this principle in our generation.

Moreover, Jesus said the defenses of hell would not be able to stand against the Church, anointed and empowered by the power of the Holy Spirit. Furthermore, He would give the Church His authority. The "keys" to the kingdom of heaven aptly symbolize the authority of the Church in the world. Note that the sphere of the Church's authority relates to the *kingdom of heaven* (spiritual things) and not to social and political movements on earth. The Church is out of its sphere when it attempts to use any other keys than those to the kingdom of heaven.

The experience of the Apostles. Jesus was anointed of the Spirit and then thrust out into the wilderness to be tested of the devil; in a very real sense, so is the Church.

Jesus spoke of the Holy Spirit's coming when He said to the apostles, "If they have persecuted me, they will also persecute you" (John 15:20). After the *anointing* of the Church on the Day of Pentecost there followed almost immediately a testing experience of persecution. Throughout the history of the Church persecution has often followed an outpouring of the Spirit. In Joel's prophecy, cited by Peter at Pentecost, he said the outpouring of the Spirit will be "Before that great and notable day of the Lord come" (Acts 2:20). It would be in the context of cataclysmic signs and worldwide upheaval.

As one reads through the Book of Acts he will see no less than five persecutions recorded in the first 12 chapters. We read such statements as these: "And they laid hands on them, and put them in hold" (Acts 4:3). "And [they] laid their hands on the apostles, and put them in the common prison" (Acts 5:18). "And they stoned Stephen calling upon God" (Acts 7:59). "And at that time there was a great persecution against the church which was at Jerusalem" (Acts 8:1).

It is equally significant that in the wake of every one of these five persecutions the Church advanced. We read such statements as these: "Many of them which heard the word believed; and the number of the men was about five thousand" (Acts 4:4). "And believers were the more added to the Lord, multitudes both of men and women. Insomuch that they brought forth the sick into the streets, and laid them on beds and couches . . . and they were healed every one" (Acts 5:14-16). "The word of God increased . . . the disciples multiplied . . . greatly . . . a great company of . . . priests were obedient to the faith" (Acts 6:7). Nothing more dramatically demonstrates the truth of Jesus' prediction that He would plant His church at the gates of hell, and the gates of hell could not prevail against it.

Nor is the story of the Book of Acts completed. Only recently in Indonesia where missionaries and Christians had been marked for martyrdom by sinister forces, there has been one of the most remarkable revivals of modern times, attended by supernatural signs such as are described in the Book of Acts. Our Assemblies of God Foreign Missions Department recently reported that during the civil war of Nigeria and Biafra, 62 new churches were started there. Since the war the Spirit has moved so mightily among churches of one major denomination that no less than 15 of them have asked to identify with the full-gospel testimony. In the language of Acts, "The Lord added to the church daily." Now, as then, the Word of God grows and multiplies in the face of persecution.

Some forces of opposition. It would be well to note some of the forms of hostility that the apostles and the Early Church faced in the heathen world. Though varied in form, these forces were motivated by the same evil one. One writer summarized, "The new faith in Christ had to *fight* its way against entrenched religious beliefs that had been in existence for centuries." The Early Church faced a hostile force in Graeco-Roman religion. The spiritual, moral, and intellectual degradation described by Paul in Romans 1 is not at all overstated. Visitors viewing the vast temple complexes at Balbek and Athens cannot but be impressed that here was a formidable force, one that captivated men's minds, their hearts, and their bodies.

The Early Church faced the intolerance of a pagan political system which moved through emperor worship to weld the world's religious loyalties to Roman political allegiance. Early Christians were branded "atheists" and were tortured and persecuted in the most cruel ways. It is noteworthy that such a union of church and state is again in store for the world. A union of religious forces will give united support to a world political ruler, whom the Bible calls the Antichrist. Present-day trends of the modern church to become overtly "politically involved" seem to point clearly in this direction.

The Early Church faced the inroads of the so-called "mystery" religions with their ritual sacrifices and emphasis upon personal experience. They stressed experience without truth, and feeling without redemption. They were "mind-liberating" and experience-centered." But they were "a gate of hell" against which the gospel of Christ prevailed. It is significant that such occultic religions are making inroads upon western society today.

The Early Church came often into direct confrontation with demonic powers in the form of occult worship. It included augury (foretelling the future), oracles, magical formulas, spells, astrology, or the reading of the horoscopes. Paul faced such forces at Philippi where he encountered the girl with the Pythian spirit, and at Ephesus with its cultic worship of Artemis. In our time we are witnessing a dangerous resurgence of such forbidden "arts," ranging from the oujia board to horoscopes.

In the intellectual realm, the philosophies held a grip on men's minds. No greater example can be cited than Paul's confrontation with the philosophers of Athens. Athens, the intellectual center of the ancient world, abounded with superstition. Here Paul's spirit was stirred within him as he saw the city wholly given over to idolatry. It was after his encounter with the philosophers of Athens that Paul wrote, "The world by wisdom knew not God, [but] it pleased God by the foolishness of preaching to save them that believe" (1 Corinthians 1:21). The apostle James used three words to characterize worldly wisdom, devoid of God as its source: (1) earthly (materialistic); (2) sensual (devoid of morality); (3) devilish (its spiritual character). He aptly describes the social behavior that is produced by this kind of philosophy: "envying . . . strife . . . confusion . . . every evil work" (James 3:15, 16). It is easy to perceive where these behavioral patterns center today—in many citadels of learning where "wisdom" is premised on a rejection of God.

Such was the world into which the fledgling Church was thrust—a world which held captive men's spirits, minds, bodies, and souls. Church historian Philip Schaff aptly puts it, "Heathenism grew wild in the soil of fallen human nature." It was the task of the Church to change this soil through the regenerative power of the gospel of Christ.

Pentecost and the mission of the Early Church. Without Pentecost the Church could never have come into being. It required the supernatural work of the Holy Spirit to overcome the obstacles set up by attitudes of people within the Church as well as those without. The Bible presents a picture of contrasts concerning the apostles and the Early Church before and after Pentecost. Their concept of the nature of the kingdom of God was changed. It is clear from the Gospels that the disciples were looking for a material and political kingdom. They were so sure of it that they were already planning details of administration: who should sit on Christ's right hand, etc. (Matthew 20:21). Hence as they ascended Olivet with Jesus for the last time, the uppermost question in their minds was, "Lord, wilt thou at this time restore again the kingdom to Israel?" (Acts 1:6). Significantly Jesus did not rule out a restoration, but He wisely directed their attention to one immediate goal: to wait in Jerusalem until they would be endued with power from on high (Acts 1:8).

Does His approach to His disciples give us direction? No one leads into truth so graciously, so winsomely, so convincingly as the Holy Spirit. Teachers should encourage their Sunday school classes to seek and wait on God for the infilling of His Holy Spirit. It will be surprising and thrilling how this resolves their "hang-ups" and changes their entire outlook! The issues and the things of this world grow strangely dim, in the light of Christ's glory and grace.

The unity of the disciples was once marred by bickering and personal ambitions; but we see their lives transformed. Let's take an example. The scene was on the highway to Jerusalem. Passover was coming. Jesus knew this would be His last journey. Already burdened by the imminence of His death, He took the Twelve aside and began to tell them what would happen to Him. Then, for some unexplained reason, the brothers James and John approached Jesus and rendered their request, "Grant unto us that we may sit, one on thy right hand, and the other on thy left hand, in thy glory" (Mark 10:37). Jesus' answer was both classical and prophetic, "Can ye drink of the cup that I drink of?" Their ready answer was, "We can."

History was to provide them just that opportunity. James was the first of the Twelve honored to lay down his life in martyrdom outside the gates of that very city where Jesus drank the cup of His suffering. John would live to be an old man with flowing white hair, but he too would taste the cup of bitterness and experience the baptism of suffering. When he wrote of his Patmos vision, he identified himself as "your brother, and companion in tribulation, and in the kingdom and patience of Jesus Christ" (Revelation 1:9). And when he had seen Jesus in His glory, all thought of earthly thrones faded and he fell at his feet (Revelation 1:17). As we examine the Gospel that bears his name, we find him so shadowed by humility that he declines to mention his own name, referring to himself only as "the disciple whom Jesus loved" (John 21:20).

The "one-accordness" (literally, "one-themness") of Pentecost would displace disputes as to "who should be the greatest" (Mark 9:34). Humility, simplicity, and openness like that of a child would characterize their attitudes. Peter and John, whose personality traits were opposites, would be used as a "team" to minister healing and the good news concerning Christ at the gate Beautiful in the Temple. In Acts 2 the apostolic company is described as being in "one accord"—a term which is repeatedly used of the Early Church (used eight times of the young church in the Book of Acts). It is a word which in the Greek expresses intensity of feeling. Such feeling could only focus in love upon the Person of Jesus, whom the Spirit came to reveal and to glorify.

It would be in Christ that Jew and Gentile would find union in Christ's earthly Body, the Church. The one-accordness which today's professing church seeks through ecumenical means will never be realized except in the manner in which the Early Church realized it—through submission to Jesus as Lord and through the work of the indwelling Holy Spirit.

The sectarian spirit ("we-four-and-no-more attitude") of the disciples, steeped in Judaistic exclusivism, yielded to a passionate and zealous missionary spirit, motivating the apostles to carry the gospel to Jew and Gentile alike. It is significant that the name changes from disciples (learners) to apostles (sent-ones). They would be sent to the uttermost parts of the earth under the Spirit's guidance. In the language of Paul, we read such expressions as "Woe is unto me, if I preach not the gospel" (1 Corinthians 9:16); and, "I am debtor both to the Greeks, and to the Barbarians . . . I am ready to preach the gospel . . . at Rome also" (Romans 1:14, 15). The missionary movement of the Early Church would make an impact upon the world from Jerusalem to the shores of the western Mediterranean world in the west, and to the shores of the Indian and Pacific oceans in the east—literally unto the "uttermost" parts of the earth.

The personalities of the disciples, once marked by timidity, vacillation, uncertainty, and political ambition, would be dynamically changed by the coming of the Spirit on the Day of Pentecost. Peter, who vacillated between daring swordsmanship and sputtering denials all in one night, became unctionized with powers of mind and speech which defied human analysis. He spoke with such prophetic insight and clarity from the Scriptures that his words made an unforgettable impact on the nation. It was a fitting demonstration of the Holy Spirit's power in persuading men. No company of men ever underwent so radical a change. No more do we hear of them expounding their aspirations for a political restoration of the kingdom of Israel. They became preoccupied with the kingdom of heaven. To them the kingdom of God became infinitely more than meat and drink; it was "righteousness, and peace, and joy in the Holy Ghost" (Romans 14:17).

It is interesting that references to the kingdom occur 116 times in the Gospels, but only eight times in the Book of Acts and six of these have to do with speaking or preaching about the kingdom of heaven. In all of Paul's epistles it occurs but 13 times, and in the other epistles only twice. In Hebrews it occurs but twice and in Revelation, five times. The point of this summation is that Pentecost produced in these men a preoccupation with the *King* of glory and less preoccupation with a material kingdom.

The apostles did not lose sight of a coming kingdom of glory, but reigning would come after *suffering* (2 Timothy 2:12). A roll call of the apostles shows that each learned the meaning of suffering, that all except one suffered a violent death. Having suffered for Christ, they will yet reign with Him. Jesus told them that there would come a day when they would eat and drink at His table in His kingdom and would sit on thrones judging the 12 tribes of Israel (Luke 22:30). In his Patmos vision, John was given a preview of thrones upon which those that were "beheaded for the witness of Jesus, and for the word of God . . . [will sit and reign] with Christ a thousand years" (Revelation 20:4). God has a way of rewarding those who put His interests first. Often it is in terms of highest meanings attached to those things they forsake in this life to serve God.

The dynamic change described above came about because of simple obedience to one simple instruction: "Tarry . . . until" (Luke 24:49). Herein lies the starting point for the mission of the Church today.

The Mission of the Church for Today. The Church still ministers in a hostile world. The same spiritual forces the apostles faced exist today in modern counterpart. Though often polished and sophisticated by culture and learning, they are nevertheless the "gates of hades" behind which many are incarcerated. The gates of this world system can and shall no more prevail against a Spirit-empowered Church in the 20th century than in the first century. But the *spiritual* nature of the Church's work must be recognized from the start. Paul said, "For we wrestle not against flesh and blood, but against principalities, against powers, against the rulers of the darkness of this world, against spiritual wickedness in high places.

Wherefore take unto you the whole armour of God" (Ephesians 6:12, 13). "For though we walk in the flesh, we do not war after the flesh: For the weapons of our warfare are not carnal, but mighty through God to the pulling down of strongholds." (2 Corinthians 10:4). This is exactly the same imagery Jesus used when He spoke of the "gates of hell."

If we are to learn from the apostles, we must recognize the hostility of the Church's working environment and the spiritual nature of its approach and resources which it employs offensively and victoriously.

The second picture to emerge from this study is the absolute necessity for a continual Pentecost in the Church today. Today's popular church is making much the same mistake as did the disciples before Pentecost—seeing its mission as political, social, and economic. The plain implication for us is that we need a new Pentecost for each new generation in order to maintain a correct perspective on the Church's real mission in the world. To the extent that the Church loses the touch and the moving of the Holy Spirit in its midst, it loses both its power and its sense of mission in the world.

2 : Prayer and Waiting on God

"Riding through the interminable solitudes of the forest, he prayed. On his bed of straw he prayed. Retiring to the dense and lonely forests he prayed. Hour by hour, day after day, early morn and late at night, he was praying and fasting, pouring out his soul, interceding, communing with God. He was with God mightily in prayer, and God was with him mightily." These words were spoken of the early American frontiers missionary, David Brainerd. The results? Men who had been described as "heathen savages" were brought to a saving knowledge of Christ and were transformed by the power and grace of God. When they returned from convocations given to exalting Jesus Christ, their voices singing the songs of Zion reverberated through those New England forests. No exercise is closer to the pulse beat of Pentecost than prayer and waiting upon God. "Tarry until" was the very watch word of Pentecost, and it denoted infinitely more than a dispensational event. It involved waiting upon God and being in His presence as did Mary when she sat at Jesus' feet. It is a term and a practice that needs to be revived among us in these days of "hurry, worry, and bury."

Jesus and prayer. Before He called the disciples, Jesus spent all night in prayer. The calling of the Twelve was a decision and an act born in prayer (Luke 6:12, 13). In all, there are 25 recorded occasions when the words *prayer* and *pray* are associated with the earthly ministry of Jesus. The Gospels show that He prayed just before or just after the leading events of His life; it is evident that prayer was a way of life with Him. James Stalker says when Jesus arrived in a town, His first thought was the shortest way to the mountain to pray, just as others might seek out the best hotel in town.

We read such statements of Jesus as these: "And he withdrew himself into the wilderness, and prayed" (Luke 5:16); "And it came to pass, as he was alone praying, his disciples were with him" (Luke 9:18); "As he prayed, the fashion of his countenance was altered" (Luke 9:29). And as we read John 17, we sense most deeply the solemnity and sacredness of His prayer as He poured out His soul in intercession in Gethsemane, just before He was to face the ordeal of the cross. It is with the background of holy example that we examine His *instructions* to the disciples concerning prayer.

So important and vital was this subject that He devoted five of His parables to it. Two deal with *perseverance* in prayer—"praying through" (Luke 11:5-8 and Luke 18:1-8). Another two have to do with correct *attitudes* in prayer (Luke 15:18; Luke 18:9-14). Still another deals with the social basis for effectual prayer—a *forgiving spirit* (Matthew 18:21-35). These principles of prayer are to be looked for in the examples and teachings of the apostles: Peter, James, John, and Paul, as well as the entire apostolic company.

Prayer and the task of the Early Church. As the disciples viewed the staggering task of evangelism that confronted them, the natural and logical urge seemed to be to "swing into action." "Not so," said Jesus, "the first approach of the Church must be prayer." Moreover, He outlined the subject of the prayer: "Pray ye therefore the Lord of the harvest that he would send forth laborers into his harvest" (Luke 10:2). Some churches within the ranks of our Pentecostal Movement have remarkable records for the number of young people who have gone out from their midst as pastors, evangelists, missionaries, and gospel workers. Such churches have a common history: they have been *praying* churches. There is a high coincidence between prayer, the moving of the Holy Spirit, and the call of God upon the lives of young people for Christian service. The *call of God* upon men's lives for Christian ministries is inseparably connected with prayer to the Lord of the harvest. The laborers are always few in relation to the enormity of the harvest. This fact should evoke earnest and continuing prayer that the Lord of the harvest will call and send increasing numbers of laborers as the Church's day of opportunity grows late. The first approach to missions, Jesus said, is the task of the Church: prayer.

This principle was not only a matter of teaching with Jesus; it was a matter of practice. He prayed all night before He called his disciples. He told his disciples to "tarry until" they were endued with power from on high before attempting to fulfill the Great Commission. Prayer is not only requisite for the calling phase of the missionary task, but equally for the spiritual preparation of those who are called.

To be sure, "tarry until" did have a dispensational meaning since the feast of Pentecost was the 50th day counted from the feast of firstfruits at Passover. But it seems certain that in our Lord's "tarry until" instruction there was to be realized something of a discipline of the spirit necessary to receiving the Holy Spirit on the Day of Pentecost. In the Old Testament when God was about to do something special in Israel's midst, His instruction was "sanctify yourselves." In other words, set yourselves apart from the ordinary routine of life to prepare spirit, mind, and even body for what God is about to do. This principle has not changed, notwithstanding a popularized push-button theology on the receiving of the Holy Spirit. We need to emphasize the art of worship and of waiting on God. "Tarry until" implies this principle also. It is one that pays rich spiritual dividends.

The Practice of the Apostles. One writer said that prayer was to the apostolic Church the very secret of a life "hid with Christ in God" (Colossians 3:3). It was to them the most natural thing in the world to pray for guidance when perplexed, for strength and blessing when the will of God was manifest. When they were about to choose a successor to Judas, they prayed (Acts 1:24). The church at Antioch prayed before they sent forth Barnabas and Saul on their first missionary journey (Acts 13:3). When Paul was kept in prison, he sought earnest prayer of the Church. When Peter was imprisoned in Jerusalem, the Church prayed (Acts 12:5). Before Pentecost they prayed (Acts 1:13, 14). After Pentecost they "continued steadfastly in the apostle's doctrine and fellowship, and in breaking of bread, and in prayers" (Acts 2:42). The very last utterance of the Spirit and the Church in the Bible is one of prayer: "Even so, come, Lord Jesus" (Revelation 22:20).

The Temple was the first center for apostolic praying. Jesus said it (His house) was to be a "house of prayer." This statement no doubt takes meaning from the time when Solomon dedicated the first temple. It was an edifice dedicated in prayer. It was to be a house wherein God said He would hear from heaven the prayers of His people when they humble themselves, pray, and seek His face, and turn from their wicked ways. Moreover, it would be the place for the forgiveness of their sins and the healing of their land (2 Chronicles 7:14). It was the place where the Shekinah glory of God came down in the midst of the praises of His people.

The apostles clung to the Temple as "the house of prayer." They observed the prayer meeting schedule in that house. The third hour, an hour of prayer, was marked by the outpouring of the Holy Spirit (Acts 2:15). The ninth hour, also an hour of prayer, saw another miracle take place, the healing of the lame man through the ministry of Peter and John—who were on their way to prayer. Even though he was away from the Temple, Peter was found in prayer atop Simon's house in Joppa at the sixth hour, or at noon. Then God gave him the vision of the great sheet with all manner of four-footed beasts and other creatures, instructing him to "slay and eat." This prepared him for what God was about to do in the Gentile house of Cornelius. In each instance there is a manifestation of the supernatural in connection with the prayer meeting or the prayer meeting hour; the apostles were in prayer or were going to prayer.

Cottage prayer meetings, as they are popularly called today, were also a part of the apostolic pattern. The prime example of such praying by the Early Church is to be found in Acts, chapter 4. "And when they had prayed the place was shaken . . . and they were all filled with the Holy Ghost, and they spake the word of God with boldness" (Acts 4:31). The Book of Acts emphasizes the power and efficacy of the body ministry in prayer. It is a principle of praying that finds it roots in the soil of Jesus' instruction: "Where two or three are gathered together in my name, there am I in the midst of them" (Matthew 18:20). Again, "If two of you shall agree on earth as touching any thing that they shall ask, it shall be done for them of my Father which is in heaven" (Matthew 18:19). There are a number of instructive suggestions in this description that relate to what the apostle James taught on prayer. There was a spirit of urgency. There was a vocal crying out to God with "one accord" (Acts 4:24). James said, "The effectual fervent [literally, the energized prayer, energized by the Holy Spirit] prayer of a righteous man availeth much" (James 5:16). This was the kind of praying Jesus did. The writer to the Hebrews said of Him, "Who in the days of his flesh, when he had offered up prayers and supplications with strong crying and tears unto him that was able to save him from death, and was heard in that he feared" (Hebrews 5:7). This portrays what intercessory prayer is.

Practically every picture of prayer in the Book of Acts emphasizes the power of group-praying and presents a scene of a lively prayer meeting involving the church as a group. Pentecost itself was in the setting of a prayer meeting. The Church continued as a body in prayers (Acts 2:42). At Antioch the Christians "ministered to the Lord, and fasted" (Acts 13:2, 3). The Early Church practiced the injunction to pray one for another on an intense scale, as the Book of Acts depicts. James' instruction on prayer was in the context of the Body's ministry to one another not only for healing but for the welfare of the total man. Note the descriptive words to describe each need situation: "afflicted" (depressed, discouraged) James 5:13; "sick" (James 5:14); and "faults" (James 5:16). The old-fashioned Methodist class meetings, which followed public services, approached such a ministry of believers to believers. There is a great need to revive such a ministry in the church today. "Pray one for another" was not just an apostolic teaching but an apostolic practice. The believer's prayer for Peter in prison is an example that could be followed in any congregation where a "prison" experience may be a difficulty, discouragement, or problem facing some member of that body. This principle could be practiced and taught in the Sunday school class by encouraging members to express their needs, then all going together in concerted prayer for that need. The pressures and the complexities of these days call for such concern and prayer for one another, and there are tremendous spiritual resources for believers to do just that.

There is yet a third level of praying practiced by the Early Church, that of the prayer closet. Peter was *alone* in prayer at Joppa when he was given that noonday vision—prayer that was preparing him for ministry at Caesarea in the house of Cornelius. In Romans 15:30 Paul asked his friends to "strive" with him in prayer. While the place of prayer is not mentioned, Paul seems to suggest intercession in the prayer closet. It was such a prayer ministry that Epaphras exercised (Colossians 4:12). This kind of praying follows the instructions of our Lord when He spoke about secret prayer in the closet—and no one knew the meaning of praying alone more than Jesus. Many of us have early and sacred recollections of our mother's or other loved one's voices coming from the closet of prayer.

The organization itself of the Early Church enhanced the ministry of prayer. Deacons were appointed specifically so that the apostles might give themselves continually to prayer and to the ministry of the Word. What a lesson and an example they left to the Church today! Those who minister the Word, whether from the pulpit or in the Sunday school class, must find a prayer closet somewhere in which to prepare to teach. A minister found the baptistry of his church a place where he could pray out of reach of the telephone or other interruptions. The result was that God blessed the ministry and growth of that church beyond all measure that could have been realized by programs, activism, or any other approach to the ministry.

Paul urged Christian widows to give themselves to a ministry of prayer and supplications "night and day." Our women's prayer circles have both scriptural and apostolic precedent.

The earliest paintings in the catacombs in Rome depict Christians with arms uplifted in prayer. Tertulian describes prayer among Christians of his day as being spontaneous and from the heart. Thus is the picture of the Early Church in prayer.

The Example of the Apostle Paul. After Paul had met Christ on the Damascus Road, one of the first statements made concerning him was "behold, he prayeth" (Acts 9:11). As we examine his life and his letters, there come into focus some profound insights on the subject of prayer. After his conversion Paul went to Arabia where he spent some time, possibly three years (Galatians 1:17, 18). There can be little doubt but that in the solitude of the desert he gave himself to prayer and meditation.

No writer of the New Testament so bathes his messages in prayer and instructs his converts in the theology and practical values of prayer as does Paul. No less than 10 recorded prayers are cited in his letters or ascribed to him in the Book of Acts. They mark him as a man of prayer—first, last, and always.

He prayed for instruction and grace (Acts 9:6, 11). He prayed in the midst of personal trial (2 Corinthians 12:8). But he mainly expressed intercession for the churches he founded. The subjects of his prayers for his converts are instructive to Sunday school teachers and pastors, for they express his concern for the spiritual growth of his converts. For the Ephesians, he prayed for knowledge and power and for inner fullness and knowledge; for the Philippians, it was for love, knowledge, and judgment; for the Colossians, his prayer was for the knowledge of God's will and spiritual understanding. For the Thessalonians, it was for that which was lacking in their faith. The sum total of Paul's concern for his "students" was their spiritual growth—not just an academic knowledge of the doctrines of the Church. The suggestion to us is that prayer is as much a part of our ministry as standing behind the lecture stand. Paul's praying for his converts was not a perfunctory or casual type of praying. It was "night and day praying exceedingly" (1 Thessalonians 3:10). It was intense prayer—an expenditure of himself before the throne of grace. The measure of a teacher's prayer life for his class is the measure of his shepherd heart for his class. The apostle Paul set a shining example for us.

No one so associated the ministry of the Holy Spirit with prayer as did Paul. He summoned the intelligence of the Spirit when he himself was unaware of what or for whom he should pray (Romans 8:26). He said that there is a point at which the Spirit Himself prays through the believer with groanings which cannot be articulated in language. His words should challenge us because in the same chapter he speaks of the groanings of a world around us awaiting redemption. Believers are to make themselves dispensable as a temple of prayer through whom the Spirit Himself can intercede. Paul also associated the gift of tongues with prayer and edification of believers: "I will pray with the spirit, and . . . with the understanding also" (1 Corinthians 14:15). When the Apostle said he "spoke in tongues" more than all of the Corinthians, he was no doubt recalling the ministry of the Spirit in his prayer life as well as in public utterance. This is a practical hint for Spirit-filled believers to help them in prayer. The Spirit will energize and edify them in prayer.

When the apostle Paul enjoined the Ephesians to "put on the whole armor of God," *prayer* was one of three practical synonyms for armor. Paul suggests there is power in prayer to influence political affairs; he enjoined believers to pray for kings and those in authority in the interests of peace (1 Timothy 2:2).

Paul's prayer habit led him to the prayer meeting beside the Gangites River outside of Philippi. Before the meeting was over he baptized a business woman named Lydia, together with her entire family. Thus Paul's faithfulness to that prayer meeting marked the founding of the church at Philippi. His experience in prayer did not end there. He prayed in the city jail at midnight (Acts 16:25). It is interesting to note that there he had the privilege of baptizing another entire family—that of the Philippian jailer.

Some time later when Paul wrote his letter to the church at Philippi, a city which had special status as an extension of Rome itself, he was in Rome, again as a prisoner. No doubt he thought of his experiences in Philippi. In his letter he urged moderation as a mark of public conduct except in one thing—prayer. In prayer, he advised, "Be careful for nothing." Another translation puts it, "Stop being worried . . . but always in prayer and entreaty, and with thanksgiving, keep on making your wants known to God" (Philippians 4:6). It is this context, and because of this kind of praying, that he added, "And the peace of God, which passeth all understanding, shall keep your hearts and minds through Christ Jesus" (Philippians 4:7). The songwriter captured this thought and expressed it, "O, what peace we often forfeit . . . all because we do not carry everything to God in prayer."

What an impact Paul's words make when considered in the light of the circumstances in which he wrote this letter. His words bear upon our times, and how they are needed in these days of perplexity and stress—days of which our Lord spoke when He said world conditions would get so insecure that men's hearts would fail them for fear of those things which should come upon the earth. If Paul could pen such words from prison, he must have proven their truthfulness by his own experience!

Praying people will be a fortified people, spiritually, mentally, and emotionally. Their outlook on world conditions will be one of *confidence* in the Lord who governs world conditions, who is Master of the storm. In this connection, note that when Jesus outlined the signs before His return (Luke 21:34-36). He gave three practical instructions: (1) "take heed to yourself" (live a disciplined life); (2) "watch" (be alert to trends), and (3) "pray" (spiritual resources). Here is instruction that touches the whole man, body, mind, and spirit, and is directed to the discipline and well-being of believers in days of stress.

As Paul's conversion was marked by prayer, so was the close of his earthly career. As he anticipated the executioner's sword, he wrote in his final letter to his son in the faith, Timothy, "I have remembrance of thee in my prayers night and day" (2 Timothy 1:3).

Prayer and the Church Today. Our Pentecostal Movement was born in prayer. It was the conditioning influence that prepared earnest believers of various church backgrounds for the outpouring of the Holy Spirit. In a Topeka, Kansas, Bible school, it is said that there was "one room . . . dedicated to the Lord as a prayer tower. The students resorted to this room for three-hour watches. Sometimes whole nights were spent in the prayer tower. Day and night, ceaseless intercession ascended to God." The first student to receive the baptism in the Holy Spirit said, "Much time was spent in prayer every day, and all the time. On watchnight we had a blessed service, praying. . . . A Spirit of prayer was upon us in the evening. It was nearly 11 o'clock on this first of January that it came into my heart to ask that hands be laid upon me that I might receive the gift of the Holy Ghost. As hands were laid upon my head the Holy Spirit fell upon me, and I began to speak in tongues, glorifying God. The hearts of the other students were made hungry for the Holy Spirit, and they continued to tarry before the Lord."

This testimony is cited because it illustrates the place that prayer had in the birth of this Movement, just as it did in the Early Church preceding Pentecost. If our present-day Pentecostal Movement would take direction from the apostles, the Early Church, and its own pioneers, it would reaffirm and intensify its hold on prayer.

People endued with the Holy Spirit will be a praying people. A praying people will be a spiritually motivated and spiritually powerful people. They will be a witnessing people. Praying people will be a watching people.

Lord, teach us to pray.

3 : Obedience and Submission

The gigantic nose cone of the multistoried rocket was poised skyward. Steaming valves on the great space vehicle seemed like the steaming fissures in the geyser basins of Yellowstone Park. Then it happened. With explosive force a blast of white vapor and a vortex of fiery flame issued forth precisely at zero of the countdown. Anchor cables dropped and the huge "bird" began to rise into the air—at first slowly and then with increasing speed, the crackling roar and the spit of fire from its powerful engines tailing from it.

Behind this phenomenon were hundreds of thousands of calculations and hundreds of thousands of man-hours of research, planning, production, and execution of the project. Everything was directed towards a twofold end: (1) to discern the "laws" of physics governing space and space-travel, and (2) to discern the means possible within these laws to achieve the desired end.

Submission and obedience are written into the very laws of nature. The conquest of space was not possible without the most precise obedience to the laws of nature governing space and space travel. What is true in the natural realm is true in the spiritual realm. God has written into the nature of the spiritual world laws that are just as precise as those in the physical world. The principle of obedience and submission is one of them. No one discerned this principle more clearly than the apostles and the Early Church. Those who would succeed in things spiritual must be as committed to this principle as scientists and technicians are to obedience to the laws governing the physical universe. However, there is one notable difference. In the spiritual world the laboratory in which the laws of the Spirit operate is the life and the heart of the person. It is at this point that we can profit from examining the life mode of the apostles and the Early Church.

The Authority of Christ and the Early Church. From the very outset of the Early Church's existence it was well established that Christ was its Head. It was implicit in the foundational declaration of Jesus Himself, given at Peter's confession, "Upon this rock [Christ] I will build my church" (Matthew 16:18). The analogy is clear. It implies and declares His headship over the Church—a truth which is the theme of Paul's Colossian letter.

The word "obedience," as it is used in the Bible and in the apostolic writings, is a word unknown in classical Greek. Yet it is a common word in the New Testament. The word "obey" in the Bible is a contextual rendering of the verb "to hear." Thus obedience in the Bible denotes an active response to something one hears, and to hear God's Word means implicitly to *obey* it. This is why the apostle James speaks of being "doers" of the Word—not hearers only (James 1:22). One implies the other. Moreover, in the messages to the seven churches of Asia, the Spirit is said to speak to those who have an ear to hear (Revelation 2:7)—an expression denoting the willingness to obey what is said to them. The supreme example of One who heard and obeyed His Father's voice was Jesus. He was obedient even unto death (Philippians 2:8).

Turning attention to the example of the Early Church, there were two commands of Jesus that called for and were given prompt obedience. Without it there would have been no Book of Acts.

1. *The Great Commission.* The story of Acts is one of obedience. The entire book is an unfolding of the Great Commission: "Go . . . teach . . . all nations . . . baptizing . . . teaching . . ." (Matthew 28:19, 20). The very structure of the book fulfills this order: (1) Obedience at Jerusalem, chapters 2-8; (2) Obedience at Samaria and Judea, chapters 8-12; (3) Obedience unto the uttermost parts of the earth, chapters 13-28.

The word "apostle" implies a fulfillment to the Great Commission. It comes from the Greek *apostello*—"I send," and is thus a synonym for "missionary." The apostles were the "sent ones" and the Book of Acts could as well be called, "The Acts of the Missionaries." The underlying principle is one of obedience. Jesus Himself was the great Missionary. He repeatedly spoke of Himself as the Messenger sent by the Father to a lost world. "As my Father hath sent me, even so send I you" (John 20:21). Forty-two references in the Gospel of John alone it is said Jesus was *sent*. He exemplified the Great Commission before He ever gave it. His claims were authenticated not only by who He is, but by His example and life of obedience.

The obedience of the apostles to the Great Commission is remarkable when one considers their Jewish backgrounds. Until Pentecost they studiously avoided contact with Gentiles. When Peter was given the vision of the great sheet let down out of heaven, his reaction was an instinctive, "Not so, Lord." But he yielded to the voice of the Spirit and later said, "The Spirit bade me go" (Acts 11:12).

When the apostles ended their earthly careers, they were in the "uttermost parts of the earth," just as Jesus had commanded them. Mark tells us, "They went forth, and preached everywhere, the Lord working with them, and confirming the word with signs following" (Mark 16:20).

History and tradition show where "everywhere" took them in obedience to the Great Commission. After Stephen's martyrdom in Jerusalem, James was beheaded by Herod Agrippa (Acts 12:2). Philip, though not one of the apostles, shared in their obedience and ministry; he is said to have been imprisoned and then crucified in Phrygia in A.D. 54. Matthew is said to have been slain with a halbert in A.D. 60 in the region of Parthia. James the Less, at the age of 94, was said to have suffered death from beating and stoning of the Jews in Jerusalem. Matthias was said to have been stoned and beheaded at Jerusalem. Andrew was said to have been crucified in Asia. Mark is said to have been dragged to pieces in Egypt. Peter is said to have been crucified head down in Rome. Jude was said to have been crucified in Asia Minor in A.D. 72. Bartholomew was said to have gone to India where he was cruelly beaten and crucified by idolaters. Thomas was also said to have preached the gospel in India and was martyred with a spear by enraged pagans. John is said to have been the only apostle to die of natural causes, but his life was spared miraculously when he was cast into a cauldron of boiling oil; later he was banished to Patmos where he received his vision of things to come; John ended his career in Ephesus.

Obedience carried with it the very real threat of death—so much so that the very word for "witness" (Greek, *martureo*) became synonymous with *martyr*. The apostles breathed the spirit of Paul who said to the Ephesian elders, "Neither count I my life dear unto myself so that I might finish my course with joy . . . to testify of the gospel of the grace of God" (Acts 20:24).

2. The principle of obedience is seen in the response of the apostles to Jesus' command to "tarry until" (Luke 24:49). They built no shrines on the spot from which Jesus ascended into heaven. They rather rallied to the practical task of *obeying* His final instruction—to wait in Jerusalem until they should be endued with power from on high. ". . . They worshipped . . . returned to Jerusalem with great joy . . . were continually in the temple, praising and blessing God" (Luke 24:52, 53). They leave us this lesson: True worship is always followed by *obedience* to Jesus' commands.

How often in the Scriptures is fidelity to God tested by simple waiting! Here is a grand example. Their obedience in waiting is related to the statement of Peter: "And we are his witnesses of these things; and so is also the Holy Ghost, whom God hath given to them that obey him" (Acts 5:32).

Some specific examples of obedience in the Early Church. The obedience of the Early Church is also seen in a number of specific circumstances.

1. They were obedient in *proclaiming an unpopular message.* It must be remembered that the Early Church existed, during the first decades of its history, within the folds of Judaism. The message of Christ crucified and resurrected was offensive to Jewish religious leaders. They were charged with guilt for the crucifixion of Christ. Their reaction was immediate and violent: "Being grieved . . . they laid hands on them" (Acts 4:2, 3). "They gnashed on him [Stephen] with their teeth . . . cried out with a loud voice . . . ran upon him . . . cast him out . . . stoned him" (Acts 7:54-58). It was in this context, incidentally, not in civil disobedience, that Peter declared, "We ought to obey God rather than men" (Acts 5:29). Not only was the message of the Cross offensive to Jews, it was offensive to the pagan world. Paul said it

was "foolishness" to the Greeks. And it was a "stumbling-block" (scandal) to the Jews (1 Corinthians 1:23).

In the Pedagogium, one of the imperial palace buildings of ancient Rome, was found a wall graffito depicting the body of a man with the head of an ass on a cross. Below the worshipful form of a young man nearby, were scratched the words, "Alexandemos worships his god"—a mocking caricature of some young Christian. It gives testimony to pagan reaction to the Cross as "foolishness."

2. They were obedient to the voice of the Holy Spirit in their ministry. Peter and John were prompted by the Holy Spirit when they stopped suddenly and ministered healing to the lame man at the gate Beautiful (Acts 3:4, 6). Philip responded in obedience to the voice of the Spirit when he left the scene of an outstanding city-wide revival in Samaria to go to the desert to minister to one person, the Ethiopian Eunuch (Acts 8). Peter, contrary to his Jewish upbringing, gave explicit obedience to the voice of the Spirit when he went to a Gentile house in Caesarea to minister (Acts 10). Peter obeyed the voice of the Spirit by rebuking the donors of a gift to the Church for lying to the Holy Ghost (Acts 5:3). The Church at Antioch obeyed the voice of the Spirit in sending out Barnabas and Saul on the first missionary journey (Acts 13). Paul obeyed the Spirit, who forbade him from going to Asia (Acts 16:6). He obeyed again when the Macedonian call by a night vision came to him (Acts 16:9). The first Church Council in A.D. 50 sought the mind of God and obeyed it in making a critical decision so that it could be said, "It seemed good to the Holy Ghost and to us" (Acts 15:28).

3. They were obedient in dealing promptly and forthrightly with sin. Again, the account of Ananias and Sapphira illustrates the seriousness with which they viewed

sin "in the camp." They turned back "gifts" rather than commercialize on spiritual gifts at Samaria. Peter told Simon, "Thy money perish with thee" (Acts 8:20).

In every case where the Church obeyed the Spirit's voice there was a clear sign vindicating the Word, with signs following. There is not a single chapter in the Book of Acts or a single letter written by the apostles which does not in some way reflect the principle of trust and obedience. It was with them a way of life. In the New Testament the word *obedience* carries the special meaning of submission to the will of God. It is a word used repeatedly of Christ (Romans 5:19, Philippians 2:8, Hebrews 5:8.)

The Apostle Paul and Obedience. When the apostle Paul met Christ on the road near Damascus, his response was immediate and complete, "Lord, what wilt thou have me to do?" His first word, "Lord," was an acknowledgment of Christ's lordship and mastery over his life. It was so from that moment until he entered into His presence some 30 years later on another road leading out of the city of Rome, the Via Ostiensis (marking the scene of his execution). By using this title "Lord," Paul acknowledged Jesus as chief, leader, or captain, and he himself as a servant. His letters deserve special study on the theme of the lordship of Christ (especially Colossians).

When Paul stood before Agrippa in a Roman court in the port city of Caesarea, he gave testimony of his Damascus Road experience. He looked back upon his life from a point when the end of his earthly career was not far away, and testified, "Whereupon, O king Agrippa, I was not disobedient unto the heavenly vision" (Acts 26:19). Obedience to the call and the will of God brings a sense of satisfaction nothing else in life can bring. Paul's path, from the Damascus Road to the scene of his martyrdom on the Ostian Way outside of Rome, was one of continuous obedience to the heavenly vision and to the call of God upon his life.

The Apostle Peter and Obedience. No more beautiful and descriptive words can be found in Scripture than those which speak of the call of Peter and Andrew: "... He [Jesus] called ... they left ... father ... servants, and went after him" (Mark 1:20). Peter's path from Galilee to Auger Vaticanus (across the Tiber outside of Rome where tradition holds he met a martyr's death in the circus [race track] of Nero), was a pathway of obedience. He had run the race with patience and obedience.

Some have appealed to Peter's words, "Men ought to obey God rather than men," to justify civil disobedience; but they do so out of context. Peter's controversy in Acts 5 was with religious "modernists," not civil authority. They were especially "grieved" over the apostles' teaching on the resurrection—a tenent the Sadducees vehemently denied (Acts 4:2).

On the contrary, the apostles taught the necessity of obedience to civil authority. Peter called Christians children of obedience (1 Peter 1:14). Peter, who once sought to take the "law into his own hands" by pulling his sword to defend Jesus in the Garden of Gethsemane, learned humility and submission, even to the point of suffering the cruel death of crucifixion (John 21:18, 19).

As we read Peter's letters in his later years we observe in him a submissive and mellowed spirit. He could encourage his readers, in the face of persecutions from Imperial Rome, to "rejoice, inasmuch as ye are partakers of Christ's sufferings" (1 Peter 4:13). It is especially worthy of notice that Peter encourages civil obedience in the face of suffering "for the Lord's sake" (1 Peter 2:13).

Peter was to experience the full meaning of these words. The Roman Tertullian wrote that Nero was the first to prosecute "this doctrine" and that he had Paul beheaded in Rome itself, and Peter crucified. Ironically, these who said, "Honor the king," (1 Peter 2:17) were to be tested by paying a supreme price for the truth they taught and lived.

The Early Church and earthly authority. In summary, the apostles and the Early Church held that man comes under four primary authorities, each requiring obedience:

1. *Parental authority.* Paul said, "Children, obey your parents in all things: for this is well-pleasing unto the Lord" (Colossians 3:20). Modern psychology is rediscovering the benefits of discipline. Psychologist Dr. Clyde Narramore writes, "The most confused and unhappy children are those who have no reasonable, consistent discipline. . . . Limits bring security and create a frame of reference for life within which a child can work or play at his best." An eminent child psychiatrist, Dr. Joseph D. Noshpitz, in a recent article charges that "a home that has no taboos, that makes no demands, that requires no politeness or conformity, that sets no firm rules and limits, is a home that the city sanitary inspector ought to serve a ticket to. It's an unhealthy place." The late Dwight D. Eisenhower, reflecting on the "stern discipline" under which he had been reared as a boy, said that the tension, fears, and frustrations of the atomic age demand an even greater internal discipline if we are going to keep from being pulled apart.

The apostles and the Early Church stood on sound ground, Biblically and psychologically. What is "well-pleasing" to the Lord is also best for the well-being of child and parents.

Among the social signs Paul listed for the "last days" (days he characterizes as "perilous"), he includes "disobedient to parents" together with "unthankful," and "unholy." This triad of terms characterizes altogether too many in affluent American homes today. They directly relate to a degenerative "subculture" movement in our land.

It would be wise to point up to our young people the Biblical and prophetic significance of the social trends in the world today. It would also be wise to point up the practical relationship of the Spirit-filled life and the undergirding strength of the Word of God as an inner defense against the spirit of the times.

2. *Obedience to spiritual leaders.* The early Christians recognized authority in the Church. "Obey them that have the rule over you" (Hebrews 13:17) was written of pastoral and spiritual leadership in the Church. Further, "Submit yourselves [unto them]: for they watch for your souls." There is the practical benefit of "soul care" for those who will obey this scriptural instruction. What is true of pastors is true of the Sunday school teacher-pupil relationship. The teacher can have a "watching" ministry over the souls of his class. This is a ministry that goes much beyond the perfunctory task of teaching a class each Sunday.

3. *Obedience in business relationships.* This is a principle equitable with honesty today. "Servants [employees], be subject to your masters with all fear; not only to the good and gentle, but also to the froward" (1 Peter 2:18). As a former businessman, Peter must have known something of employer-employee relationships. He was speaking of a social system that denied many people. Angus said that ancient Roman society rested

on the foundation of slavery—something that could not be suddenly abolished without plunging society into chaos. The historian Gibbon estimates that one-half of the Empire was in a state of slavery. Le Maistre puts the figure up to 60,000,000. Slaves had no rights or protections from the brutality of their masters. Augustus is said to have crucified Eros, his steward, for eating quail. Roman ladies are said to have torn their attendants' faces or to have driven pins into their flesh if a curl was out of place. Yet it was in this setting that the apostles enjoined obedience to masters.

4. *Obedience to civil authority.* We have cited the example of Peter and civil authority, but what was the position and general teaching of the Early Church? It seems clear that the Church's stance was primarily related to God and not to government for the latter's sake. There is also every evidence that the Church suffered because of its position, and "beastly" and cruel men in seats of authority took advantage of the Church. Yet Paul said, "Let every soul be subject unto the highest powers." Then in very strong language Paul said that God deals sternly with those who resist civil authority. They will receive to themselves "damnation" (Romans 13:2). Paul himself worked within the *system* when he availed himself of the legal appeals provisions, right up to the supreme court of the empire. He exercised the privileges of his citizenship at Philippi when he was unlawfully beaten. Again he acknowledged and worked within the *system* when he met Onesimus, a runaway slave in Rome, and sent him back to his master in Colosse. The word and spirit of the Scriptures and the attitude of the Early Church are not compatible with the "civil disobedience" philosophy of some clergy and churches of today. Submission to God carries with it a

commitment to "submit yourself to every ordinance of man *for the Lord's sake*" (1 Peter 2:13).

The practical implications of obedience and submission for today. In his Ephesian letter, Paul related obedience and submission to the *Spirit-filled life.* It was after he gave his imperative, "Be filled with the Spirit," that he detailed the *social implications* of being "filled with the Spirit": "Submitting yourselves one to another in the fear of God. Wives . . . unto your own husbands . . . Husbands, love your wives . . . Children, obey your parents . . . fathers, provoke not your children . . . Servants, be obedient to . . . masters . . . masters, . . . forbearing threatening" (Ephesians 5:18 to 6:9). Of all people, Paul suggests that Spirit-filled people should exhibit obedience and submission in the family, the church and the world. The indwelling Holy Spirit is a resource of grace, strength, and motivation for a becoming Christian walk.

Obedience is not only linked to the Spirit-filled life in the teachings of the apostles, it also is linked to the development of Christian character. The classic statement comes from the writer of Hebrews: "Though he [Christ] were a Son, yet learned he *obedience* by the things which he suffered" (Hebrews 5:8). God's view of discipline is the response of believers to *obedience.* It has been wisely said, "Adversity is like a storm. It drives some ships to destruction, and it drives others to harbor." Both Paul and Peter could testify to the relationship of divine discipline to learning obedience. Paul told the Corinthian church, "Most gladly therefore will I rather glory in my infirmities, that the power of Christ may rest upon me" (2 Corinthians 12:9).

Finally, obedience and submission have *missionary implications* for the Church today. Suppose the apostles and the Early Church had *not* obeyed the Great Commission. Suppose the apostle Paul had *not* been obedient to the Macedonian call which brought the gospel to Europe and the Western World. Could it be that we in our hemisphere would be living in the degradation, filth, and superstitions of jungle tribes? How we should thank God that the apostles and the Early Church did obey! Their obedience has made us eternal beneficiaries of the gospel. One writer has pointed out that the term *missions* implies three essential factors—the sender, the one sent, and the one to whom sent (Romans 10:10-15). In each the underlying principle is obedience. The collective response of local churches and the individual responses of individuals in our churches make up the middle link in this chain of obedience to our Lord's Great Commission.

Our Lord and the apostles told us plainly that the current of attitude and thinking in the end time would be *against* a spirit of submission and obedience. Jesus said because "iniquity [literally, lawlessness] [would] abound, the love of many [would] wax cold" (Matthew 24:12). He added, "If ye love me, keep my commandments" (John 14:15). His rebuke of the church at Ephesus was because they had left their first love (Revelation 2:4). Jesus' corrective prescription for this condition was "repent and do the first works" (Revelation 2:5). Here is a practical approach to obedience and submission where the motivating force of love has waxed cold.

4 : The Spirit-Filled Life

The Six-day War of June 1967 had come to a climactic and dramatic halt. The barriers forbidding Jews access to the "Old City," Jerusalem of Bible times, had come down. The several blocks of hovels that formerly filled the Tyropoean Vale to the west of the wall had been cleared away by bulldozers to make way for a great convocation. Then 200,000 Jews gathered in front of the Wailing Wall—the spot religious Jews have held to be the most sacred spot on earth since the time of the destruction of their temple in A.D. 70. One observer reported seeing men, women, and children praying before that wall, kissing the huge stones and crying in response to deep emotions pent up within.

The victorious Israeli nation had just been through a battle as miraculous and spectacular as when the nation marched around the walls of Jericho some 3,400 years before. When the chief rabbi blew the *shofar* (ram's horn) at the Wailing Wall (just as the priests blew the *shofar* at the walls of Jericho), his words were, "This year in Jerusalem, ancient Jerusalem!"

The Holy Spirit has been peculiarly associated with the restoration of Israel as a nation. This part of the prophetic process deserves special study. It was the vital force of the Holy Spirit that revived Israel from the slumber of death when Ezekiel in a vision saw the nation become a "living army" (Ezekiel 37). It was the Spirit of

God that assisted Zerubbabel when in the face of great opposition he undertook to rebuild the Temple at the nation's first restoration. There the Spirit gave him the familiar promise, "Not by might, nor by power, but by my spirit, saith the Lord of hosts" (Zechariah 4:6). Thus the Spirit of God is instrumental in both the political and the spiritual restoration of Israel. It is interesting that orthodox Jews today hold that the Spirit of God has never departed from the western wall of the Temple courtyard, the Wailing Wall.

The Coming of the Holy Spirit and a "New Nation." Another event of miraculous character also took place during the Feast of Weeks (Pentecost) in approximately the same location as the event we have just described. It happened almost 2,000 years ago. A new "nation" was born in a day—not a political nation, but a spiritual nation of believers known as the church of Jesus Christ. Peter described the Church as a "holy nation, a peculiar [set apart] people" (1 Peter 2:9). Just as the Spirit of God brought together natural Israel in the face of tremendous odds and opposition, so He caused the birth and has continued the life of spiritual Israel—the Church. Let us never forget that the Church is a *miracle* wrought by the Spirit of God, that it is sustained by the same power that brought it into being!

The world was steeped in pagan darkness when the Holy Spirit came, when the sound of a mighty rushing wind and flaming tongues of fire burst upon the heads of that waiting company of 120 in the upper room at Jerusalem during the Feast of Weeks nearly two millennia ago. In the beginning of time, when the earth was "without form, and void," the Spirit of God moved upon the face of waters and brought order out of chaos. So at Pentecost He descended upon a world fraught with the chaos of sin and moral disorder to bring order and harmony in lives of men. His instrument would be a mere handful of men and women gathered in an upper room in Jerusalem.

Forty days had passed since Jesus of Nazareth had been crucified by orders of Pontius Pilate. Sholem Asch describes the scene: "As the feast of Shevouth [Weeks] approached, the hosts of the Ebionim, the poor, the homeless and the forlorn streamed into the city with its winding, crooked streets, terraced by steps and lined with shops and alley-side dwellings. They attracted little attention, as Jerusalem was accustomed to the spectacle of groups of families, and sometimes even entire villages, coming into the city for a sojourn of several weeks. Slipping in among the festive crowds that filled the city were the followers of Jesus of Nazareth." The role these humble Galileans were to play in theirs and succeeding generations could hardly be anticipated by their outward appearance.

This being the time of the great festival of harvest, the pilgrims brought with them offerings to the house of God. Every province sent fruits and vegetables which had ripened earliest within its territory—figs, beans, or sheaves of grain. Sholem Asch further describes the festive mood of the occasion, in some respects not unlike our traditional county fairs. He tells how every group came marching in to the sound of flutes and timbrels with an ox, or some other sacrificial offering adorned with costly ribbons, or whatever else the offerer could afford. Perhaps it is with this feast in mind that the apostle Paul makes the association between the Spirit and the "fruit" of the Spirit.

Pentecost was the most joyful of all Jewish festivals. Many came just to witness the colorful ceremonies, to prostrate themselves in worship and to hear the Levites blow their silver trumpets or to play on their harps while singing from the Psalms. Others would watch the white-robed priests stand barefooted before the altar, offering up the sacrifices prescribed for the feast. The sea of pilgrims clad in bright and colorful clothes made a spectacular sight.

But on this occasion the unexpected occurred. At nine o'clock in the morning there came a sound of a great windstorm upon one company of people sitting by themselves. Just as suddenly there burst upon their heads what appeared to be flames of fire. These were the same phenomena the nation had witnessed some 1400 years before at Sinai when Moses ascended the Mount and the nation of Israel was born. The Law was written then on tables of stone, but now it was written by the Holy Spirit as a transcript of God's moral nature on the fleshy tables of men's hearts. (See Exodus 19, 20.) The third phenomenon is familiar to us: They all "began to speak with other tongues, as the Spirit gave them utterance" (Acts 2:4).

The news of this strange event spread rapidly throughout the city, bringing pilgrims in masses to the scene where the 120 were gathered. As the milling crowds increased, a burly fisherman stood up to speak, and his voice rang out with the clarion tones of a trumpet. He told the crowd something that sounded incredible. Jesus of Nazareth whom they had crucified at Passover just seven weeks before, was none other than their Messiah; and He was alive. This meant they should repent and believe on Him. Three thousand responded.

The Holy Spirit's Ministry Through the Early Church. The *power* of the Spirit is demonstrated here in His principal office work in the world, that of backing the gospel message in convicting power upon unbelievers. "They were pricked in their heart, and said unto Peter and the rest . . . Men and brethren, what shall we do?"

(Acts 2:37). Jesus had told them that when the Spirit came, "He [would] reprove men of sin, and of righteousness, and of judgment" (John 16:8). It was concerning the *Person of Christ* that the Spirit convicted the 3,000 who responded in saving faith that day. Just as Jesus came to reveal and glorify the Father, so the Spirit came to reveal and glorify the Son. Here was evidence of His convicting power, relating to the hearts and minds of men.

The power of the Spirit is demonstrated in healing ministry at the gate Beautiful of the Temple (Acts 3:7). This healing (as are all healings) was not an end in itself. It attested that Jesus was indeed resurrected and alive, that He continues to minister to human need through His church. Peter had told them that Jesus was indeed the Messiah, and this healing proved it. Among the prophecies concerning the Messiah was that the "lame man shall leap as an hart" (Isaiah 35:6). The Acts record said of this lame man, "And he leaping up stood, and walked, and entered with them into the temple, walking, and leaping, and praising God" (Acts 3:8).

The power of the Spirit is demonstrated in the personal enduement of individuals for witness. Where they were deficient He qualified them intellectually, psychologically, and physically. This was clearly demonstrated in the experience of Peter and John at the Temple when they were called before the rulers. The Bible says, "Now when they saw the boldness of Peter and John, and perceived that they were unlearned and ignorant men, they marvelled" (Acts 4:13). The experiences of the apostles have been repeated time and again in the lives of such men as Smith Wigglesworth and other stalwarts in the history of the Pentecostal Movement.

True boldness is not the same as a personality "quirk."

Wigglesworth was prevailed upon to visit and pray for a lady of considerable wealth who was ill. One witness said,

> We drew up at the door, rang the bell, and were ushered into a palatial room. From there we moved into a very large bedroom. There, like an eastern monarch on a throne sat the gorgeously robed lady in a rainbow-colored pile of . . . cushions. Wigglesworth stood and was startled at such a sight. Then he said, "Well! You certainly look comfortable!" "I beg your pardon," she snapped. "I said you look very comfortable!" She let loose in a storm of abuse which left her exhausted. "Oh!" he said, "I can see that you are not ready for me yet. Good evening." He walked out of the house and into a waiting automobile.
>
> After he had left her, she repented. God healed her and at the morning service the next day she publicly consecrated her life to God. She was a broken woman, profuse in her apologies. One minister who had thought Wigglesworth rude said, "We had been wrong in our judgments and God had vindicated Smith Wigglesworth's action."

The apostle Paul testified that his speech and his preaching was not with enticing words of man's wisdom, but in *demonstration of the Spirit* and of power (1 Corinthians 2:4). What applies to preaching is equally true of teaching. It is doubtful if Peter, the Galilean fisherman, or even Paul, the Tarsian tentmaker, were polished orators. Yet they communicated with an unction of wisdom and power that penetrated men's hearts and influenced their choices for God. Many Sunday school teachers communicate in a "low key" manner as far as oratory is concerned; yet there is an unmistakable penetrating unction of the Spirit that ministered beyond their words to their hearers. These are individuals who know the meaning of the prayer closet as well as diligent study of God's Word when they prepare their lessons.

The power of the Spirit sustained the Early Church in times of persecution. Jesus told the disciples that the

Spirit would be to them a *Comforter* (literally, a *Paraclete,* "one called beside"). We should notice that He spoke of the coming Comforter in a context of coming difficulty and persecution: "If the world hate you, ye know that it hated me before it hated you . . . But when the Comforter is come . . ." (John 15:18, 26). Throughout the Bible the Holy Spirit came on the scene and gave enablement and power in the face of *difficulty.* This is a theme worthy of special study. It is demonstrated time and time again in the lives of the apostles and the Early Church. Recall that it was at a cottage prayer meeting in Jerusalem where prayer was made in behalf of Peter in prison that there came a shaking visitation of the Holy Comforter (Acts 4:31). Stephen was marvelously sustained by the Holy Spirit while he was being assaulted by a violent mob that could not gainsay the words and wisdom given him by the Holy Spirit (Acts 7:55).

The fires of persecution could not put out the fire of God that burned within the hearts of those early Christians. The flames of fire that sat upon the heads of the 120 on the Day of Pentecost became symbols of zeal and the spreading character of the Early Church. When the Bible says "they that were scattered abroad went every where preaching the word" (Acts 8:4), it was like scattering hot coals of fire through tinder-dry forests. The holy flame that started in Jerusalem was spread through the "uttermost parts" of the earth within one generation of time.

The Holy Spirit *guided* the Early Church, as individuals and as a body. The Spirit guided the evangelist Philip to the most unlikely place to witness to a lone traveler in the deserts of southern Palestine. Philip was bid of the Spirit to "join himself" in conversation with the Ethiopian Eunuch (Acts 8:29). The Spirit guided him in his witness: "Then Philip opened his mouth, and began at the same scripture, and preached unto him Jesus" (Acts 8:35). Incidentally, there are many sincere people who leave a church service and as the Ethiopian Eunuch need the witness concerning Christ brought to them. The Holy Spirit is zealous concerning the Person of Jesus and will use a yielded vessel to witness to a hungry soul concerning Him. It was the Spirit who conveyed Philip away to another city, when his mission had been completed (Acts 8:39).

It was the Holy Spirit who bade the prophets and teachers at Antioch to separate Barnabas and Saul for the work to which He had called them (Acts 13:2). It was the Holy Spirit who guided the first council of the church at Jerusalem so that it could be said in conclusion, "It seemed good to the Holy Ghost, and to us" (Acts 15:28). It was the Holy Spirit who guided Paul and Barnabas, forbidding them to enter fields which they had considered (Acts 16:6, 7), and then calling them to enter Macedonia (Acts 16:9).

How wonderful to be able to trust the Holy Spirit for such guidance! The Spirit's direction is always consistent with the Word of God and with the commands of Christ. The Word and the Spirit complement each other in guiding the believers. Jesus promised that when the Spirit came He would guide believers into all truth. We can believe He meant truth not only as a doctrinal proposition, but truth in the sense of knowing and doing the will of God.

It is said that at the beginning of the Jewish war the Early Church was prophetically warned by the Spirit to leave Jerusalem and migrate to Pella, a Gentile city in Transjordan. The fate of the city in the summer of A.D. 70 is attested by the Jewish historian, Josephus. Had the Church remained in the city, it would have shared in the bloodbath which the city experienced at the hands of Titus and the Roman armies.

When the apostle Paul speaks of the Holy Spirit's guidance *in prayer* (Romans 8:26), there can be no doubt but that he knew the meaning of what he wrote from his own experience. Without ceasing Paul prayed in the Spirit, and we have only to read the letters he wrote to his converts to know that the Spirit laid them continually on his heart.

The Holy Spirit ministered in *edification* to the Early Church. This is the thrust of the apostle Paul's teaching on the gifts of the Spirit. Validated by love, they minister strength, encouragement, and warmth. The attitude of the Early Church as evidenced in the writings of Paul deserves our prayerful attention. "Concerning spiritual gifts . . . I would not have you ignorant" (1 Corinthians 12:1). Ignorance of the resources of God's grace and of His Spirit can be costly. The Christian congregation on the Isthmus of Corinth, beset by the baseness of paganism, buffeted by dark spiritual forces, and trampled upon by a debased and sensual commerce, needed the inner ministry of the Holy Spirit to emancipate it from such depressing and demonic pressures. Notwithstanding their errors, it is to their eternal credit that they sought for the resources of the Holy Spirit. Even their mistakes have left us a spiritual heritage in the correctives which the apostle Paul gave in the Corinthian Letters, penned under the guidance of the Spirit. "Covet earnestly the best gifts," he said. God wants us to seek earnestly the gifts of His Holy Spirit, which when conditioned by love, take on an abiding quality. "Desire spiritual gifts," the apostle urged as the yearning mind of the Spirit was expressed from his heart and his pen. How often we tend toward relegating the gifts of God's Holy Spirit to the closet. As if the Spirit were in contest with human pride, Paul further warned, "Quench not the Spirit. Despise not prophesyings" (1 Thessalonians 5:19, 20). An omniscient Holy Spirit knew the human tendency to relegate Him to a "back room" in the name of doing "things decently and in order." In so doing, we risk the loss of His edifying ministry; and we risk grieving Him. Let us not do it. We cannot afford to be without Him.

The Holy Spirit and the work of the Church today. The familiar story *Acres of Diamonds* illustrates a truth which may be especially relevant to us today. A man in South Africa aspired to seek his fortune in diamonds and sold his farm to set out around the world in search of diamonds. After some years he returned in vain, not finding the object of his search. In the meantime the new owners of the property discovered on it one of the richest diamond mines in the world.

Could it be that we tend to go in search of diamonds when God has planted us as a Movement on one of the richest spiritual "diamond mines" in the world? If we will follow the wisdom and the example of the apostles, we will soon recognize that we have resources in the Person of the Holy Spirit Himself that could "turn the world upside down" in our generation.

The most subtle thing about spiritual inertia and loss is insensibility to it. This is why the apostles emphasized being continually filled with the Spirit. It is stated on three occasions that Peter was filled with the Holy Spirit. Being filled with the Holy Spirit is no one-time-only experience as confirmation or water baptism. One of the most striking words to be found in the Book of Acts is the word "continued." "They continued stedfastly in . . . doctrine and fellowship, and in breaking of bread, and in prayers . . . and they, continuing daily with one accord in the temple, and breaking bread from house to house . . .

praising God" (Acts 2:42, 46, 47). As long as the Church *continued*, the Lord *added* to the Church. Not only were the apostles filled with the Holy Spirit on the Day of Pentecost, but they were *again* filled with the Spirit in the wake of the first persecution (Acts 4:31). If we follow out the implications of Paul's statements, we will see that they were filled again, again, and again like a continual flow of water from a living spring. The verb tenses of the apostle in Ephesians 5 are worth noting: "Keep being filled with the Spirit." "Stop getting drunk on wine." "Keep on praying in the Spirit." Being filled with the Spirit is within the volitional grasp of believers. The Bible never instructs to do that which we cannot.

In like manner the exercise of the gifts of the Spirit are within the volitional grasp of the believer. Twice Paul told Timothy to "Neglect not the gift" within him (1 Timothy 4:14) and to "stir up the gift of God" imparted to him with the laying on of hands (2 Timothy 1:6). As pastors and Sunday school teachers we can take instruction from the apostle and encourage our youth to seek and to exercise the gifts of the Holy Spirit, to continue in the exercise of the Spirit's ministry. One of the snares to be recognized here is a "graduation psychology" with reference to the infilling of the Spirit. In the same vein, Paul instructed Timothy to "meditate" and to take heed unto the "doctrine," that is, the Word of God. The Spirit and the Word are compatible channels through which God works in the lives of men. The qualities of the Spirit-filled life in Ephesians 5 are identical to the list in Colossians 3, describing the life in which the "Word of Christ" indwells richly.

Being filled with the Spirit is never a luxury any more than the weapons and armor are to a soldier in battle (Ephesians 6). As the battle lines of spiritual conflict are becoming more intensely drawn, the necessity for the Pentecostal enduement is ever more urgent; the frustrations of the modern church without the resources of the Holy Spirit are too obvious for any other conclusion.

The mission of the Pentecostal Movement is not to be "just another denomination." It is to be a witness to the world in the last days of what God can do through men yielded to and filled with His Holy Spirit. Our greatest contribution to the world is simply to be what God raised us up to be: to be Pentecostal in the apostolic sense of the word.

So never underestimate the impact of the Spirit-filled life of the teacher in the Sunday school class. It communicates a lesson that is often more effectively demonstrated and radiated from the life of the teacher than could be taught any other way.

5 : The Christ-Centered Life

The morning sun shot its rays to Hebron in the distance and beyond. As the massive gates of the Temple slowly swung open, the sound of silver trumpets blown by the priests awakened the city to the dawn of a new day. Within the courts of the vast temple complex were busy preparations for the day. The stone towers of the Fortress Antonia silhouetted the sky adjacent to the temple precincts like a giant architectural sentinel symbolizing law and order. On the heights of the western hill and overlooking the "ditch," called the Tyropoeon Valley which divided the city, were the apartments of the high priest's palace. Before this day would pass, something unusual would take place there.

The day wore on to the mid-afternoon, and the hour approached for the prayer meeting at 3 o'clock. The worshipers poured in through the gates, finally ascending to the highest level of the courtyard. One gate was far more magnificent than the others. The gate itself was made of dazzling Corinthian brass, richly ornamented. Its double doors were so massive that it required 20 men to open or close it. But something in the scene was wrong. On the steps was a familiar figure, a man crippled from birth, so much so he had to beg to sustain even a pitiful existence. Among the crowds passing up those steps to the stately gates were two Galilean fishermen. Suddenly these two stopped in their tracks as if transfixed by some unseen force. They stopped not to give him alms, but yet they stood there with fixed gaze upon a helpless form and upon a hopeless face that pleaded for pity. Then one of them uttered words this man had never heard before, "In the name of Jesus Christ of Nazareth rise up and walk."

What followed reveals that Christ was indeed alive and that the followers of Jesus of Nazareth were still very much in company with Him. As the apostles put forth their hands and pulled him to his feet in the name of Jesus the Nazarene, a burst of strength and energy transformed that crippled body from impotence to wholeness. It was the power and the impact of the resurrected Christ ministering through the lips and hands of the apostles.

As the evening shadows began to fall over the temple court, police moved in and arrested the apostles and "put them in hold" (prison). But the effect upon the crowd had already been made; the arrest came too late. Before it was over, 5,000 men believed on the name of Jesus of Nazareth—a phenomenal response that exceeded even that at Pentecost. This compassionate ministry of Christ through Peter and John was most convincing to the multitude that witnessed this event.

One of the significant things of this incident came out in testimony at the trial the next day: "When they saw the boldness of Peter and John . . . they marvelled; and they took knowledge of them, that they had been with Jesus" (Acts 4:13). This statement signals the fact that the Central Figure in the Book of Acts is the *resurrected Christ,* working with His church, confirming the Word with signs following (cf. Mark 16:20).

We should remind ourselves at this point that the Book of Acts is a *continuation* of "all that Jesus began both to do and teach, until the day in which he was taken up" (Acts 1:1, 2). The prospects implicit in this statement are exciting. They suggest that the ministry of a miracle-working, compassionate, and resurrected Christ would continue in and through His church. In fact before He left the disciples, He told them, "He that believeth on me, the works that I do shall he do also; and greater works than these shall he do; because I go unto my Father" (John 14:12). Christ's *works* were never an end in themselves. The word for "miracle" is the same as for "sign." A sign never points to itself but to its subject. So in this incident, the focus of attention from beginning to end was upon the *person* of Jesus Christ of Nazareth, in whose *Name* the lame man was miraculously healed. The apostles hastened not only to disclaim that the healing took place by their own holiness or power, but to assert that it took place through faith in the name of Jesus Christ of Nazareth, whom the Jewish leaders denied.

The Early Church and the Person of Christ. In relationship to Christ, the Early Church was completely abondoned to His will. They obeyed His commands explicitly and implicitly. They accepted Him literally, without stopping to rationalize or to question His commands. Nothing more graphically illustrates this fact than their obedience to His command to tarry in Jerusalem for the promise of the Father; then to carry out His instructions in the Great Commission. The entire Book of Acts is structured around the obedience of the Early Church to Christ's command.

Jesus equated love with obedience, "If ye love me, keep my commandments." In this light, consider Thomas. Thomas has often been criticized for his doubts. Actually, the overriding character of Thomas was his intense *love* for Jesus. He so loved Jesus that he thought it better to die than to be bereft of His company. In the face of possible death by going with Jesus to Bethany (John 11:16), he was willing to risk that possibility if that is what it meant to be with Jesus. The announcement at the Last Supper that Jesus was about to depart filled him with perplexity: "We know not whither thou goest; and how can we know the way?" (John 14:5). His question prompted Jesus' classic words, "I am the way, the truth, and the life."

It was yet that yearning devotion to Jesus that caused Thomas to say in effect when the news of the resurrection reached his ears, "It's too good to be true. Except I touch Him, I can't really believe it!" Thomas should not be charged with a cold, calculating skepticism. Rather, he reveals a warm, intense devotion that sought the touch of the Master.

Yet this apostle, who so depended upon the personal presence of the Lord Jesus, was to experience His presence of faith as he fulfilled the Great Commission: "Lo, I am with you alway [s], even unto the end of the world." Tradition tells us he carried the gospel probably farther than any other apostle—going by foot over mountains and deserts and through valleys and jungles to carry the good news of Christ to India. His imprint is there today. The Mar Thomas Church of India attributes its founding to the apostle Thomas. He loved Christ intensely and obeyed completely.

Many times since the time of Thomas a simple, an unadorned grave in the heart of Africa, Asia, or somewhere else in the "uttermost parts of the earth," has marked the place where some missionary followed the example of Thomas. They have experienced the meaning of Jesus' promise, "Go . . . and lo, I am with you alway, even unto the end of the world." The apostles found fulfillment and satisfaction in obedience, and when the apostle Paul completed His earthly career, he could say, "I was not disobedient unto the heavenly vision."

A second fact of the Christ-centered life as illustrated by the apostles was their refusal to take glory to themselves or to commercialize the ministries God gave them. To put it another way, their first impulse was to *exalt* Christ in and through all they accomplished. Two illustrations stand out in the Acts record. Again we note the healing of the lame man at the gate Beautiful and the immediate disclaimer by Peter and John: "Why look ye so earnestly on us, as though by our own power or holiness we had made this man to walk?" (Acts 3:12).

In a similar circumstance, Paul and Barnabas at Lystra refused to accept the acclamation of being "gods" when an almost identical healing took place. They also suffered persecution and almost death as a consequence of their disclaimer. Every preacher and every Sunday school worker who experiences a measure of success faces the same test of humility and should ask God for the right heart attitude to give Jesus the glory. The commercialization of a healing ministry or any other ministry not only aborts the Christ-glorifying purpose, but actually invokes God's judgment (Acts 8:20-22).

It is reported that Evangelist Billy Graham at the outset of his ministry said, "Oh, if somehow the Lord could use me a little bit." Is this not a great part of why God can use him as He does? The apostle Paul said that "God hath chosen the foolish things of the world to confound the wise . . . the weak things . . . to confound the things which are mighty . . . and base things . . . to bring to nought the things that are," for this reason: "That no flesh should glory in his presence" (1 Corinthians 1:27-29).

Still another fact of the Christ-centered life exemplified by the apostles is that Christ was the center of their preaching. It is recorded of Philip at Samaria that he "preached Christ unto them" (Acts 8:5). Though he was not one of the Twelve, his message and ministry was representative of the Early Church. It is recorded of Paul that he "preached Christ in the synagogues" (Acts 9:20). An analysis of the apostles' letters to the churches makes it clear that Jesus was the "binding center" of what they had to say. The final book of the New Testament, brought to us from the pen of the apostle John, is the unveiling (revelation) of Jesus Christ (Revelation 1: 1, 2).

In the Book of Acts there are five speeches by Peter, and in each one Christ is central. Christ was the theme of Stephen's message before the Council, and it was Christ whom Stephen saw standing at the right hand of the throne of God. Christ was the theme of Paul's orations wherever he went. His whole message to Jew and Gentile is summarized in 1 Corinthians 1:23, 24: "We preach Christ crucified, unto the Jews a stumblingblock, and unto the Greeks foolishness; but unto them which are called, both Jews and Greeks, Christ the power of God, and the wisdom of God." The word "stumblingblock" (Greek, *skandalon*) is of the same root from which we derive our word "scandal." The message of Christ crucified was a "scandal" to the Jews, yet it is the glorious, saving message by which God has ordained the salvation of the world. The brief survey below of what the apostles emphasized in their preaching concerning Christ will be instructive.

1. They heralded Him as the *Messiah* of the Jews (the name *Christ* is the Greek equivalent to Messiah, meaning literally, the "anointed one"). Jesus Himself declared God had anointed Him: "The Spirit of the Lord is upon me to preach . . . to heal . . . to set at liberty . . . to preach the acceptable year of the Lord" (Luke 4:18). In the

healing of the lame man in the temple, Peter and John did not hesitate to press the claim of Christ as the Messiah, for this healing presented the most positive affirmation of Jesus' Messiahship according to Isaiah 53:5, 6. This demonstration of Christ's messiahship was convincing proof, and 5,000 men caught the significance of it and believed on Him. Peter pressed the point also by citing the prophecies as to Christ's suffering—a fact they had witnessed just seven weeks before.

2. They heralded Him as the *resurrected* Christ. Again and again the apostles mentioned the resurrection in their preaching. It was the central point of Peter's sermon at Pentecost (Acts 2:24, 31, 32). It was the theme of his second sermon (Acts 3:15). It was, in fact, his defense before the Jewish Council (Acts 4:2, 10). It was at the center of the apostle's preaching as a whole (Acts 4:33). It was the focal point of Peter's reply on his second arraignment (Acts 5:30). It was a vision of the resurrected Christ that was the center of Paul's conversion experience on the Damascus Road (Acts 9:3-6). It was in Peter's message at the house of Cornelius (Acts 10:40). It was the subject of the vision Stephen saw when he was stoned and saw heaven opened (Acts 7:55). The resurrection emerges in Paul's preaching at Antioch (Acts 13:30-37); at Thessalonica, (Acts 17:3); at Athens (Acts 17:18, 31); at Jerusalem (Acts 22:6-11), and before Felix (Acts 24:15, 21), and Festus and Agrippa at Caesarea (Acts 26:8, 23). The *resurrection* was at the very heart of apostolic preaching. It has often been said that the Holy Spirit is the central figure of the Book of Acts; in fact, it is the *resurrected Christ* who is the central figure of the Book of Acts. He is presented as very much alive, directing His church and working with it, confirming the Word with signs following.

The apostles demonstrated the Christ-centered life by

doing what He did—ministering compassionately to men who were oppressed by the devil. In his sermon at the house of Cornelius Peter spoke of how "God anointed Jesus of Nazareth with the Holy Ghost and with power: who went about doing good, and healing all that were oppressed of the devil; for God was with Him" (Acts 10: 38). The Church was anointed by the Holy Spirit on the Day of Pentecost for precisely the same purpose—to continue the compassionate ministry of Jesus, whose very name means "Jehovah delivers" or "Jehovah saves." How this world needs deliverance from the oppression of the devil today! The Christ-centered life is to do in His name and by the power of the Holy Ghost what He did. It was demonstrated in the lives of the apostles again and again. On the Day of Pentecost 3,000 repented and were delivered from the oppression and power of sin (Acts 2:38); at the preaching of Peter and John 5,000 were saved (Acts 4:4); at the same meeting the lame man was delivered. In the Temple and in the streets a multitude from throughout the entire region brought sick folks, and those vexed with unclean spirits, "and they were healed every one" (Acts 5:16). In Samaria the picture was the same: "For unclean spirits, crying with loud voice, came out of many that were possessed with them: and many taken with palsies, and that were lame were healed. And there was great joy in that city" (Acts 8:7, 8).

The outreach of the apostle Paul was one of ministry to human need, tirelessly carrying the gospel from city to city—reasoning, preaching, praying night and day, healing, and teaching. The Early Church went out into the market places, the highways, into synagogues, and whereever people were to be found. They were the "hands of Christ extended." When the ministry activities for which Jesus was anointed at the commencement of His ministry is studied (Luke 4:17-22), they will be seen to be identical to those fulfilled by the apostles and the Early Church. They proclaimed the message of saving faith through Jesus. They healed the sick in His name. They cast out demons. They were instruments of deliverance to men and women in spiritual, moral, intellectual, and physical bondage to the power of Satan. This ministry work list has never been withdrawn. It is still the work list for the church today.

The Holy Spirit and the Christ-centered Life. The Christ-centered life among the apostles was the product of the Holy Spirit's work in them. Nothing is more clear in the New Testament than the teaching that the Holy Spirit came to bear witness of Christ and to glorify Him. Even the gifts of the Spirit are validated by the fruit of the Spirit—the essence of which is the *Christ-life* within believers.

Jesus said that the Holy Spirit would have this work with regard to the *world*: it would be a ministry of convicting men concerning sin, righteousness, and judgment to come. Each of these categories relates to the sinner's relationship to Jesus Christ (John 16:8-11). This is illustrated in the experience of Paul before Felix. Amidst the pomp and splendor of a seaside palace at Caesarea, the apostle was ushered into the court to stand before the procurator, who himself had once been a slave. When Paul was given opportunity to speak to this man whose life and scruples were of the basest sort, he reasoned of righteousness, temperance, and judgment to come. Each of these areas was especially relevant to this man's condition. But it was more than the voice of the apostle that penetrated his ears and pierced his heart. It was the convicting ministry of the Holy Spirit, reproving him of righteousness, of judgment, and of sin. The power of the Spirit's witness behind Paul's words caused Felix to tremble. He tragically resorted to the escape mechanism of procrastination.

On the Day of Pentecost it was not merely Peter's words about Christ that convinced 3,000, and yet another 5,000 a few days later. It was the Spirit Himself bearing witness concerning Christ. The Jewish people already had the Word of God in the Old Testament Scriptures; but the results in the Book of Acts came when the Word was quickened by the Spirit, spoken with clarity by the apostles, and supernaturally confirmed by signs which attended it.

The Holy Spirit glorifies Christ and reveals Him in and through believers. As the physical life of the Church's first martyr, Stephen, ebbed away amidst the bludgeoning thuds of the stones hurled from hateful and violent hands, his countenance glowed with the radiance of another world. From a heart which was filled with Christ's love, there came from his lips the same words that Jesus uttered on the cross, "Lord, lay not this sin to their charge" (Acts 7:60). There is no doubt that the impact of this scene haunted the young man, Saul, and played no little part in preparing him for the revelation of Jesus, whom he was to meet on the Damascus Road.

Stephen was full of the Holy Ghost; and he demonstrated the graces and the love of the Christ-centered life. There is an inseparable connection between the two.

The Person of Christ and the Church Today. There are two generalizations that come out of this study of the Early Church and its relationship to Christ. They are especially relevant to us today. The first is the need to recognize the headship and authority of Christ over His church, as did the Apostolic Church. The second is the need to recognize the relationship of the Holy Spirit to the task of revealing and glorifying Christ.

The headship of Christ over the Church needs to be

recognized anew in our time's intellectual atmosphere which decries authority at all levels. Let us not think it cannot creep into our experience. It *is* creeping into the Church in various forms. It may seem simple enough to pass off the "God is dead" movement as a bit of theological faddism, but it is more than that. There are spiritual winds blowing which are anti-Christ, and thus anti-God. We may take prophetic insight as to the coming of this movement from the Bible itself. The very name *Antichrist* denotes a spirit of antagonism toward Christ. John told us that the *spirit* of antichrist was already in existence in an initial stage of ferment in the world even in his time (1 John 2:18). The end-time picture given us in the Book of Revelation is of Satan's attack, particularly directed against Christ. It is succinctly wrapped up in a single statement: "And the dragon was wroth with the woman, and went to make war with the remnant of her seed, which keep the commandments of God, and have the testimony of Jesus Christ" (Revelation 12:17).

In the last century the deity of Christ, His miraculous life and resurrection were attacked in the name of "scholarship." In our time we have witnessed such terms as "demythologizing" in reference to the Person of Christ. But we may expect a vicious and determined antipathy to develop toward Christ and His true church as the age draws to an end.

It is in the same end-time picture that the Person of Christ stands as Judge and Head among the candlesticks representing His church scattered throughout the world.

The second fact for the Church today is the Holy Spirit's witness and ministry in the Church concerning the Person of Jesus. Even as Jesus continually bore witness of the Father and glorified Him, so the Holy Spirit glorifies Jesus. But He accomplishes this in and through believers. Jesus said of Him, "I will send [Him] unto you. . . . He shall testify of me. . . . He shall glorify me" (John 15:26; 16:14).

R. A. Torrey, points out that many fear to emphasize the truth about the Holy Spirit lest Christ be disparaged. But the opposite is true. "No one magnifies Christ as the Holy Spirit does. We shall never understand Christ nor see His glory until the Holy Spirit interprets Him to us."

The writer recalls vividly his first experience in attending Pentecostal services in a little tabernacle "across the tracks" in a town in southern Washington. Such fervent devotion for Jesus Christ was found in the worship among those saints. Often the congregation would be caught up in weeping, praise, and in singing-devotion around such choruses as, "I Love My Jesus," or "Look to the Lamb of God." No visitor in those services could be unaware that there was a vital, dynamic atmosphere of worship which centered in the Person of the Lord Jesus Christ. Yet it was obviously the Holy Spirit who magnified Jesus, who revealed Him in His glory, and who inspired the love, praise, and devotion of those saints for Him.

R. A. Torrey said it so aptly: "All real beauty of character, all real Christ-likeness in us is the Holy Spirit's work; it is *His* fruit. He bears it, not we. . . . The life we all long for is the *Christ-life*. It is the Holy Spirit who produces it within the yielded believer's life. . . . Settle it clearly and forever that the flesh can never bear this fruit. We hear a good deal these days about ethical culture, which usually means a cultivation of the flesh. . . . We hear also about cultivating graces of character, but we must always bear in mind that the way to cultivate true graces of character is by submitting ourselves utterly to the Spirit to do His work."

6 : A Holy and Pure Life

If you were to visit the rolling hill country near Bethlehem, there might all of a sudden leap out at you a scene from the Bible going back to the days of Ruth: an Arab farmer diligently driving his donkey in circles around on his threshing floor. This is the ancient method of harvesting grain. After this process, he would remove the straw and sweep up the residue admixture of grain, chaff, and broken stalks of grain together with other foreign materials. This would then be winnowed when the breeze was right, and sometimes the winnowing would be augmented by the use of a fan. The whole process was directed toward one end: to separate the grain from the chaff and other foreign debris mixed with it.

It was to precisely the same process that John the Baptist referred when he prophesied concerning the baptism in the Holy Spirit. It would be a baptism administered by Jesus Himself, the Lord of the harvest. "Whose fan is in his hand, and he will thoroughly purge his floor, and will gather the wheat into his garner; but the chaff he will burn with fire unquenchable" (Luke 3:17). The language and the analogy suggest a connection between the coming of the Holy Spirit and His purifying work in the lives of those whom He would indwell. Just as the wind blew away the chaff and the fire burned it at the scene of the harvest threshing floor, so the manifestation of these phenomena at Pentecost suggested the purifying work of the Spirit in men's lives.

While the primary purpose of the Spirit's coming was to empower the apostles and the Early Church from on high, there is abundant evidence that He is also purposed to purify men's lives within. Our Holiness friends emphasize the work of the Holy Spirit for power "to be" (holy), while we in the Pentecostal ranks emphasize His work for power "to do" (to witness). The Holy Spirit has a keen interest in both purposes. The traditional Pentecostal Movement of today has been a movement with an emphasis on holiness. A truly Pentecostal Movement could hardly be concerned with less.

The Holy Spirit and Holiness. Recently the Religious News Service carried as one of its major news stories the account of a proposal by a major Protestant denomination to liberalize its stand on "premarital sex." The spokesman being interviewed resorted to some sophisticated "double talk" (to Bible believers), calculated to reconcile modern thinking with what the Bible and the Church has traditionally held on the subject. Today's advocates of license decry "puritanism" as some outmoded vestige of "primitive ethical development in society." Yet the social, spiritual, moral, and the health problems (both physical and mental) that follow in the wake of such permissiveness are devastating. The problems with which our western society are presently preoccupied largely relate to its lost awareness of sin.

The truth that God is *holy* is a fundamental truth which the Bible declares in both the Old and New Testaments. Unlike the meaning of the term among other ancient peoples, *holy* to Israel not only meant separation from (the ordinary) and consecration, it denoted freedom from all defilement—purity. In the degraded mythology and religious concepts of the ancient Babylonians and the religious rituals of the Canaanites their deities were called "holy ones." Yet they were personifications of a fallen nature whose "worship" involved sexual vice. Greek and Roman mythology celebrated deity figures whose skills at seduction and vice were their heralded qualities. Ritual prostitution was the human enactment of what they conceived their deities to be. At Byblos, Tyre, and other Phoenician cities, "sacramental sex" was characteristic of the spring festival. Temple prostitutes, both men and women, were associated with all the temples where chambers for sexual intercourse were available. At Byblos, Lucian says that young women were expected to sacrifice their virginity in honor of Adonis and Aphrodite, and those who refused had their heads shaven. Today, bold digression from the revealed standards of God's Word in the name of "sacramental" acts is nothing short of debased heathenism, and God's judgment rests upon it as surely as it did in Bible days.

The Bible presents a God whose holiness manifests itself in hatred of sin, delights in righteousness and purity, separates the sinner from Himself, and punishes the sinner, and manifested itself *supremely* through the death of His Son, Jesus Christ. The entire system of Mosaic washings—the divisions in the structure of the Tabernacle among the people of Israel and the Law itself—all combine to teach, emphasize, and reemphasize in the hearts and minds of God's people the truth that God is Holy, that He demands holiness in and among His people.

The relationship of the Holy Spirit to purity is revealed in His very name, the *Holy* Spirit. Of the nearly 20 names given Him in the Bible, this one by far, is the most common. It emphasizes His essential moral character. He is holy in Himself, and He imparts holiness to others (1 Peter 1:2). He is called the Spirit of holiness (Romans 1:4). His office work in the world is to convict it of sin and of righteousness and of judgment to come (John 16:8-11). Within the Church as well as without it, the Holy Spirit stands opposed to sin and judges it. Hence the symbols of purging or purifying the threshing floor of chaff and other impurities were most appropriate of His coming to the Church. The wind blows them away; the fire burns them with "unquenchable fire." It is in the light of His essential character that we now examine the fact of holiness in the Early Church.

The Early Church and Holiness. The meaning of the word translated "church" (*ecclesia*) means "called out ones" in the ordinary sense of summoning or calling an assembly; this was common in ancient Roman and Greek cities. Yet the apostles and the New Testament make it clear that the term has a special meaning as it speaks of the body of Christ. Peter declared the Church to be a "holy nation" (people) (1 Peter 2:9). Paul said Jesus died for the Church in order to make it "holy" (Ephesians 5:26; 1 Corinthians 1:2). The Church is sanctified (set apart) in Christ Jesus (1 Corinthians 6:11). In the Early Church the experience of the apostles relative to holiness was both positive and negative. We cite two examples from the Book of Acts. The first is positive.

The record for this example is in Acts 15. The sweeping impact of missionary evangelism, especially through the ministry of Paul in the Gentile world, precipitated a serious question to the young church. Should Gentile converts be circumcised and keep the Jewish Law as ordinary proselytes to the Jewish faith did? The concern and the wisdom of the Holy Spirit which led to the conclusion of the matter is instructive for us today. It draws a line between legalism and holiness without compromising holiness. Two requirements were enjoined upon Gentile converts. These we will examine.

1. *Holiness and communion with the world.* "Abstain

from meats offered to idols and from things strangled" (Acts 15:29). In Gentile centers throughout the ancient Roman world, meat was often from animals which had been offered at heathen temples. The problem was acute in Corinth. Paul instructed believers there concerning it in 1 Corinthians 8. The ancients (especially in the Greek world) held that if meat came from a sacrificial animal, to eat of it was to enter into "communion" with the deity to whom it was sacrificed. Moreover, it must be recognized that eating in the ancient Near East had connotations vastly more than nourishment. It involved communion and identification with the persons who shared a meal and often had sacred and covenant significance. In the positive vein, it is this very fact that makes the Lord's Supper so vital and significant among believers. It is identifying with Him and drawing vicariously upon His atoning work for body, soul, and spirit. It is a way of entering by faith into *His* life (1 Corinthians 10:16). It was in this context that the apostle Paul said it is possible to have communion with devils (1 Corinthians 10:21). Fellowship at the Lord's table demands separation from sin and the world and a singular dedication to Christ.

Abstaining from meats offered to idols was therefore both a matter of testimony and of spiritual communion. The practice of holiness in *abstaining* has multiplied applications for us in the light of this twofold truth. The things we partake of spiritually, intellectually, and physically all have communion connotations, for better or for worse. Abstaining from the things of the world has testimony implications (this is important), but the *spiritual* implications are just as real. The apostles taught that communion (not communication) with the world and communion with Christ are not compatible. For us the question of "meats" can be practically equated: (1) What impairs my testimony, and (2) what impairs my communion with

Jesus Christ is bad for me. The places we go, the things we watch, the things we read, the company we keep—all have communion implications. To be filled with the Holy Spirit implies cultivating a sensitivity to sin and a spirit of discernment with regard to these things.

It was precisely on this point that the church of Pergamos was troubled. The church had cooled off spiritually and received the Lord's rebuke in the Book of Revelation (Revelation 2:14).

Added to meats in this prohibition were "strangled things." Strangled things had peculiar efficacy in heathen eyes because they did not shed blood, and thus did not call for "vengeance from the ground." They also held that strangled things had a magical influence—a concept which still exists in some parts of the world.

While the Early Church seemed to be specially concerned with testimony and communion, it should also be added that God's concern with men's diets is at these two points. Paul decried the use of wine because indulgence robs men of spiritual power. But the principle is not confined to wine only (Ephesians 6). He too expressed concern about believers' dietary habits and testimony. He chargd the people of Crete for carelessness in diet and with laziness, and he instructed Titus to "rebuke them sharply" that they may be "sound in the faith" (Titus 1:12, 13). The Spirit-filled life is a disciplined life. The apostle Paul testified that he kept *under* (controlled) his body (1 Corinthians 9:27).

2. *Holiness and moral life*. "Abstain . . . from fornication" (1 Thessalonians 4:3). It is here where the apostles and the Early Church had the most to say about purity. It was by some ironic twist that the title "holiness" was applied by fertility cult devotees to their deity figures, who were to them the personification of sex and war. Anath, for example, in the Canaanite system was called

Qudshu, "the holiness." She was goddess of sex and war. When the writer visited ancient Balbek in Lebanon, he noted the two most prominent sculpture figures in that vast complex to temple ruins were the egg (symbolizing sex and fertility) and dagger (symbolizing death, relating to war).

While talking with another minister on the plane from Beirut to Athens, the writer called attention to the relationship of these two elements in society today. They are indeed very much tied together in today's world. An age of permissiveness in sex has also been related to unprecedented and continuous engagement in warfare ever since World War I. It is noteworthy that the apostle James tied "lust" and "war" together. While he uses the word in the context of material things, in the broader context it connotates self-gratification, whether in acquiring things or satisfying appetites (James 4:1-5). Our "sexplosion" and our "explosions" of war are not accidental corollaries. They represent man's uncontrolled depravity and his desperate need of regeneration.

The purity demanded of the Early Church stood in sharp contrast to the pagan world. There is no sin so repeatedly condemned in the Word of God as was fornication. Paul's sharpest words of rebuke to the church at Corinth were for its laxity at this point. "What? know ye not that your body is the temple of the Holy Ghost . . . ?" (1 Corinthians 6:19).

The Bible speaks nothing of a "sex education" apart from moral purity. One has but to examine some of the statements of the spokesmen and philosophers of those times to know that the *status quo* was one of impurity. Cato, according to Horace, looked on fornication (prostitution) as a preventative against libidinous intrigues with married women. Cicero says fornication was *always* practiced and allowed. It was defended as "customary and as necessary." The Roman Emperor Severus furnished his governors with concubines. Cynic and early Stoic philosophers among the Greeks excused fornication on the ground of "doing what comes naturally." The apostles refuted such pagan morals on the ground of the importance of the sanctity of the body as the temple of the Holy Ghost. Both the Lord Jesus and the Holy Spirit have a vested interest in the bodies of believers. They are to be kept pure from defilement, whether it be in the flesh or in spirit, perfecting holiness in the fear of God (2 Corinthians 7:1). Paul said that for Christians to engage in prostitution (illicit sex) was a desecration of God's temple. We should see it as blasphemous and vile as that of Antiochus Ephiphanes when he offered a sow, an unclean animal, upon the altar of the Temple in Jerusalem.

The Early Church stood firm against fornication in every form. At Corinth where a thousand *hiero-douloi*, or "sacred" prostitutes, from the hill-top sanctuary of Aphrodite flooded the streets with their nefarious traffic among sailors, merchantmen, and townspeople, the problem was acute. But there was no accommodation to it by the Church. The awesome catalog of moral degradation described by Paul in Romans 1 could well have been observed by him at Corinth. The word was "flee fornication" (1 Corinthians 6:18). It still stands today. A believer who fails to purge himself of it cannot be "a vessel unto honour, sanctified, and meet for the master's use" (2 Timothy 2:21).

3. *Holiness and honesty*. The Early Church also placed high value on truthfulness and honesty. The Holy Spirit is called the "Spirit of Truth," and lying to the Holy Spirit invoked a fatal judgment upon Ananias and Sapphira (Acts 5). God neither smiles nor winks at exaggerations. The proverbial "evangelistically speaking,"

whether it be in reference to reporting crowds and response at a revival service or the amount of the sale on a piece of property, ought to be a term antonymous with absolute honesty and truthfulness. The glory for accomplishment in giving in the apostolic church belonged exclusively to God Himself. The Holy Spirit is sensitive to truth and to honesty. It is no more compatible for Him to indwell a temple that is involved in contrivance against truth and honesty than in a temple defiled by prostitution. Someone has said, "If God dealt today the way He dealt with Ananias and Sapphira, there would not be enough people left to sing the doxology in some churches." The fact is, God will deal with every person and every church according to the standards of truthfulness with which He dealt with those two; but not always with the same swiftness.

The apostles had something to say about honesty to the churches to whom they wrote: "Let us walk honestly . . . not rioting and drunkeness, not in chambering and wantonness, not in strife and envying" (Romans 13:13). The apostles taught that honesty is a way of life connected with being "law-abiding, quiet, and peaceable." As a matter of testimony, Paul urged the Thessalonians to "walk honestly toward them that are without" (1 Thessalonians 4:12); and to the Romans, "provide things honest in the sight of all men" (Romans 12:17).

James, Apostle of Holiness. If we could single out one apostle whose life and words are representative of what the apostles practiced and taught on holiness, it could well be James. The Bible gives us but a fleeting glimpse of him. Paul calls him one of the "pillars" of the Church (Galatians 2:9). He is the brother of Jesus and one to whom Jesus made a special appearance after His resurrection. He was leader and chief spokesman at the Apostolic Council (Acts 15).

James' personal character is revealed largely by his epistle. He was a "holiness preacher." He insisted on a standard of holiness in the use of the tongue (James 3:2-12; 4:2, 11). His standard of holiness insisted on refraining from unkind judgments of one's neighbor (3: 14; 4:11), of making rash oaths (5:12), or of obsession for money and wealth (5:1-6). His standards of holiness banned favoritism in the church based on a man's station in life, bank account, or clothes (2:1-13). His standards of holiness decried a wisdom that failed to display the marks of purity, peaceableness, gentleness, mercy and good fruits without partiality and without hypocrisy (3:18). His standards of holiness decried wealth gained through fraud or "driving a hard bargain" upon employees. He advocated a standard of holiness which makes one unafraid to confess faults and sins and which puts a man on effectual praying ground with God (5:16).

From all that is known about James he practiced what he preached. He was highly regarded not only by Christians, but also by unbelieving Jews. Josephus, the Jewish historian, says he was put to death by the high priest in A.D. 62. Eusebius says that James was surnamed "the Just" by the ancients because of his eminent character.

Holiness and the Church Today. From a study of Satan's attacks upon Israel, it soon becomes apparent that the nation's greatest vulnerability was from within. Before the nation ever set foot in the promised land, a noted magician, named Balaam, was engaged by Israel's enemies to put a "hex" on them. His formula was not to oppose Israel from without but to corrupt the nation from within. The Bible calls this "Balaam's doctrine." It worked. No fewer than 24,000 perished. Incidentally, the form of the seduction was along lines of sexual impurity—the same thing that later plummeted the nation to ruin by entanglement with the fertility cult religion of the Canaanites. In the Book of Revelation the Holy Spirit calls for the Church to remember the error "the doctrine of Balaam" (Revelation 2:14). In Pergamos a number of teachers were advising Christians to participate in a "new morality" philosophy and doctrine. It brought Christ's rebuke and God's judgment.

What Israel was as a spiritual institution in the Old Testament, so is the Church in the New Testament. Purity and holiness are very much related to the church's *effectiveness* in the world today.

The roots of our Pentecostal Movement are deep in the soil of holiness. The imprint of holiness is perhaps one of the most distinguishing marks upon us as a Movement. Many of the pioneers of this Movement were men of deep convictions and on holiness of life, whatever their denominational backgrounds might have been. It could hardly have been otherwise with men who have come into contact with the purifying flame of God's Holy Spirit.

Let us make no mistake about it. The sharpest attack of Satan against Pentecostal people will be to get them to *broaden* their viewpoints and become more tolerant of worldly currents of thinking and practice. We used to hear from our pulpits warnings against compromise. Perhaps it is time to restore it to our vocabularies.

We are witnessing a day when the spirit of the world decries *separation* at any level of life. The clamor is to remove any and all lines of distinction that separate society. This trend is expressed in ecumenism, amalgamations, and federalization at every level of life: political, religious, social, and economic. The trend has very definite implications for the Church today, just as it did for the Early Church in the days of the imperial persecutions of Rome.

As this trend ripens, we may expect to witness a growing polarization within the Church as a whole and a growing hostility between the spirit of the world and the spirit of Christ as they move towards the climactic battle which the Bible prophetically describes. The apostles gave us some definite clues and trends for which to look as we see this process develop. Peter described some teachers as "false prophets . . . who privily shall bring in damnable heresies . . . as natural brute beasts . . . having eyes full of adultery, and that cannot cease from sin; beguiling unstable souls: an heart they have exercised with covetous practices; cursed children: . . . following the way of Balaam, the son of Bosor, who loved the wages of unrighteousness" (2 Peter 2:1, 12-15). Strong language? Yes, but apt and accurate language.

Harold J. Ockenga, in an article, "Who Is Tampering with the Church" (*The Pentecostal Evangel*, April 9, 1967), put his finger on the current trend when he pointed out that the underpinings of the "God is dead" movement are really rooted in an attempt to do away with *absolutes* (the idea that there is a precise line of demarcation between right and wrong, or good or bad). And along with this teaching came the "new morality." According to this idea, all ethics are "situational" and "relativistic," and they must be governed by the "eternal attribute of love"—a term which however pious-sounding, to these people makes each person, and not God's Word, the judge of what is "right or wrong." It is the same twist of reasoning that emerged in the dialogue between Satan and Eve in the garden; God's instruction, "Thou shalt not eat of it" (an "absolute"), was replaced with the ethic of "situational" judgment. Satan said discernment as to what is good and evil would be transferred from God to men: "Ye shall be as gods, knowing. . . ." Here is a good example of departing from literal obedience to God's Word; this is precisely what some teachers are advocating as a standard of conduct today. The source is the same now as it was then.

The Book of Revelation presents two figures representing two contrasting movements in the world. One is a *bride*, pure, chaste, clothed in clean and white garments, awaiting the wedding and the marriage supper of the Lamb. The other is a *harlot*—whom God judges. God's eternal standard of life for the Church is "follow . . . holiness, without which no man shall see the Lord" (Hebrews 12:14).

7: Evangelism and Witnessing

Envision the scene described in the first chapter of Acts. We may see a slow and deliberate procession moving up the long pathway from the Kidron Valley to the summit. The Master is surrounded by the familiar figures of the apostles. They edge their way up the path until the vast panorama of the Jordan Valley to the east bursts into view. Beyond that the terrain of the rolling plateau country fades like a vast beige-colored ocean of land. More immediately in the foreground the scene looks down upon a little village called Bethany, glistening in the Palestinian sun on the slopes of Olivet. It is colonnaded with trees whose graceful fingers point toward heaven as if to declare, "He is risen," in prophetic suggestion of the momentous event about to take place.

Jesus has just finished saying something to the group that milled about him; suddenly a mystic cloud of glory appears and envelopes Him. The little group is startled, for their Master begins to move up away from them and then disappears in the cloud. Transfixed by awe and amazement, they stand speechless and dazed, looking into heaven. Suddenly their gaze is brought back to earth by two men who appear in their midst, asking them why they are staring into heaven. The two then announce that this same Jesus would return in the same manner as they had just seen Him go.

As the awe and benumbing daze of that moment begins to wear off, the Master's last words come back to them, "But ye shall receive power . . . ye shall be witnesses unto me . . ." (Acts 1:8).

Ascension, descension, and extension—these three words tell the story of the Book of Acts. In Acts 1 it is *ascension;* in Acts 2, it is *descension* (of the Holy Spirit); and from the hour of the Spirit's descent it is the record of *extension.* This third word is associated with the word Jesus had just given them before He disappeared from their view—"witnesses."

What is remarkable about Jesus' statement here is the precise geographic pattern in which this witnessing was fulfilled under the Holy Spirit's direction: (1) in Jerusalem, Acts 1-7; (2) in Judea and Samaria, Acts 8-12; and (3) "unto the uttermost part of the earth," Acts 13-28. There is a very real sense in which this pattern emanates again and again from each center of witness. Today the mother-church concept coupled with a strong missions program gives reenactment of the Acts pattern, within and from each community where there is a gospel witness.

The Meaning of Witness and Evangelism. Two words in the New Testament, "witness" and "evangelism," need to be examined to get a better picture of the Early Church as it carried out the Great Commission of the Lord. Witness relates to the *messenger;* evangelism to the *message.*

The term "witness", as it is used in the Bible, had a number of meanings. In the Old Testament it often denoted a memorial. Jacob raised a heap of stones called "the heap of witness," between himself and Laban to mark the boundary between them. It was a tangible expression of an agreement or an event. Near ancient Dothan is a heap of stones, erected as a memorial to the Israeli soldiers who died in battle at that spot during the 1967 Six-Day War.

In the Law of Moses the term "witness" referred to prosecuting an offender, and witnesses were the first executioners (Deuteronomy 13:9; Acts 7:58). But in the New Testament the idea of a witness is one who attests his belief in the gospel by personal suffering.

The Example of Stephen. The Holy Spirit paints for us a picture of the Church's first martyr. He is first described, together with the seven deacons, as a man "full of the Holy Ghost and wisdom." He gives pointed demonstration of these qualities in the story that follows. His words and deeds were attested by the power and authority of the Holy Spirit. He did "great wonders and miracles among the people" (Acts 6:8). In his synagogue dispute with the Jews, "They were not able to resist the wisdom and the spirit by which he spake" (Acts 6:10). They resorted to perjury and bribes to build a case against him.

As reason gave way to mob violence, Stephen was dragged from the city to a spot that is today identified as St. Stephen's Gate. There he sealed his testimony with his blood. Stephen's story has been repeated time and again by saints throughout the history of the Church.

In the confirmation of the gospel message, the New Testament appeals to two kinds of witnesses—human and divine: (1) the witness of *believers* to Christ, and (2) *God's witness* concerning Jesus by "signs following." In Acts 14:3 and 15:8 miracles are taken to be the means by which the preaching of Christ among the Gentiles was so attested (cf. Galatians 3:5).

Jesus told the apostles that since the world persecuted Him, they could expect similar treatment. Hence the word *martyr* is translated "witness" in a number of passages and expresses the active hostility of the world toward the gospel message (Matthew 5:11). Early Christians enjoyed a degree of immunity from direct Roman control so long as it was thought by Rome that they were one and the same with Judaism. Yet under Nero imperial policy changed, and the fiercest of persecution was waged against the Christians. The Neronian persecutions form the backdrop of the letters of 1 Peter and 2 Timothy. It is worthwhile to study these two letters of the New Testament in that light. The Roman historian Tacitus tells us that in the wake of the great fire in Rome in A.D. 64, Christians were made the "scapegoat" for Nero's crime. In and around the city Christians by multitudes were arrested and put to death in the most cruel ways. Some were crucified; others were tied in skins of animals and thrown into the arena to be worried to death by dogs for the *entertainment* of the people. Others were thrown to wild beasts; some were tied to stakes in Nero's gardens and then used as human torches to light his gardens at night. Nero would then drive about in his chariot, naked, indulging himself in his midnight revels, gloating over the dying cries of his victims. For Christian women it is reported that the brutalities were even more dreaded than death.

It is commonly believed that in the wake of this persecution Paul was arrested again, tried as a criminal (cf. 2 Timothy 4:2-9), condemned and executed. Certainly 2 Timothy presents a picture of Paul as a condemned prisoner in "death row" awaiting execution.

Hence when we think of the word *witness*, its meaning as experienced by the apostles is intensified by Peter; he described the adversary's rage like the fury of a lion stalking his prey; and that stalking was happening all over the Roman world. These early Christians found the resource and comfort of fellowship with Christ in His sufferings. It was in this context that Paul said, "If we suffer, we shall also reign with him: if we deny him, he also will deny us" (2 Timothy 2:12). Tradition holds that Peter was put to death by crucifixion in the wake of the same persecution that took Paul. The tradition is a persistent one, cited by historians Clement, Ignatius, and Eusebius.

Members of the imperial family itself did not escape martyrdom. Believers were charged with atheism when they accepted Christ. Atheism in that context was to refuse to worship the emperor of Rome. Emperor Domitian's own cousin, Consul Flavius Clemens is reported to have been condemned for being a Christian and was put to death. His wife Domitilla was banished to Pontia. The blood of the martyrs was indeed the seed of the Church.

Thus a witness was one who gave *testimony* concerning Jesus Christ. The witness was one often called upon to suffer persecution or even seal his testimony with his own blood.

The Meaning of Evangelism. The *evangel* and the *gospel* have the same meaning. In its simplest meaning it is "good tidings," and it speaks forth the *message* of the Church. It is missionary in its implications. *Tidings* can be tidings only to those who have not heard them before, and they can be *good* only to those who receive and act upon them. It was upon these tidings that the apostles premised their declaration: "For whosoever shall call upon the name of the Lord shall be saved" (Romans 10:13).

The gospel was declared by Paul as "the *power* of God unto salvation to every one that believeth" (Romans 1:16). It is literally the miraculous power of God, wrought through the agency of the Holy Spirit to everyone who believes. It is the same miracle-working power that supports the "signs following" those who believe. God supports the preaching of the gospel, and at the point that it is believed something miraculous happens. God honors no other message in this way, and this is why it is absolutely necessary that the message of the Church be the gospel—whether it be given in the Sunday school, from the pulpit, or by door-to-door witnessing. This is demonstrated time and time again in the witnessing of the apostles, as we shall see.

The Example of the Apostles in Proclaiming the Gospel. Examine the elements of Peter's witness on the Day of Pentecost. At the heart of it is the simple but penetrating story of the death, burial, and resurrection of Jesus; it is issued in a call to "repent and be baptized." This was exactly as Jesus prescribed in His Great Commission (Matthew 28:19, cf. Acts 2:22-38). Consider the elements of Peter's second witness in the Temple, and the same elements are seen to emerge (Acts 3:14, 15). Again it ended with a call to repent. God honored it and 5,000 men believed. In Peter's third witness (Acts 5:29-32) the same elements emerge. In this instance his hearers responded negatively; and God held them responsible for their rejection, even warning them through one of their own spokesmen, Gamaliel (Acts 5:30-39). Stephen's message brought to bear on the same thesis (Acts 7:52-56). In his martyrdom he even updated the evidence for the resurrection of Jesus by declaring that he saw Him at that moment, as the heavens opened, standing there in full view on the right hand of the Father (Acts 7:52-56). Note the elements of Philip's witness to the Ethiopian eunuch: He preached unto him Jesus as the fulfillment of Isaiah's great prophecy on the Suffering Servant (Acts 8:30-35). At Samaria Philip's message was Christ. God backed it up with signs following: miracles, healing those with unclean spirits, healing sick bodies, healing depressed spirits (Acts 8:5-8). Examine Paul's first recorded message at the mountain city of Psidian Antioch. The heart of his message concerns the death, burial, and resurrection of Jesus with a call to believe in him (Acts 13:27-37).

The word "proclaim", used 120 times in one form or another in the New Testament, describes the means by which the apostles communicated the evangel (the good news concerning Christ). It is a word that carried the meaning of both publicity and authority (power). Paul told the Corinthians that God has ordained that it is through preaching (proclaiming) that God saves them that believe (1 Corinthians 1:21). Moreover, it is the preaching of the *cross*, a term which encompasses the saving mission of Christ in His death, burial, and resurrection—there is to be found the saving power of God (1 Corinthians 1:18).

Witness and evangelism to the apostles were inseparably connected with heralding the good news concerning Christ. The apostles knew no other message. They presented no other name or authority by which men could be saved. God honored no other message than the gospel of Christ. The Church's charter authenticates no other message or mission. In fact, Paul said any other gospel invokes God's curse, even though it might come from an "angel in heaven" (Galatians 1:8).

Channels of Evangelism in the Early Church: Men. E. M. Bounds wrote, "God's plan is to make much of the man, far more of him than anything else. Men are God's method. The Church is looking for better methods; God is looking for better men. When Paul appeals to the personal character of the men who rooted the gospel in the world, he solves the mystery of their success."

If the Biblical record and subsequent history make anything clear, it is the fact that God has chosen to use *men,* uniquely equipping them with power to do His will. There is a sense in which, like Adam, God formed the Church from the clay of humanity. The disciples were the clay. On the Day of Pentecost God breathed into them the breath of life, and the Church became a living soul to bear witness of Jesus Christ's creative power and saving grace.

When the angel appeared to Cornelius at Caesarea, he instructed him to send for a man, Peter, to present the gospel message. When the Church Age was inaugurated, it was in the hands of a man, not an angel, that Christ placed the keys of the Kingdom. Every time a minister proclaims the gospel and every time a Sunday school teacher ministers the Word of God they are using the God-given keys to the Kingdom. Ponder the significance of what you do when you give forth the Word of God or when you give witness to a neighbor and others.

The Apostolic Roster. The apostles named in the first chapter of the Book of Acts are Galileans—all with Jewish names except two, Andrew and Philip, whose names are Greek. Heading the list is the most dynamic and striking personality of them all, Simon Peter. As a Jewish boy he received a normal elementary education in his native village of Bethsaida. The symbol of his life as a disciple is his boldness, yet in the end, his cowardice. He walked on the sea. For a moment we see him striding on the top of the wave; the next instant he is shrieking with terror, "Lord, save me!" He professes loyalty to Jesus beyond his brethren; he draws the sword in the face of great odds in the garden; yet he wavers before a servant girl and denies the Lord. He was never at a loss for words—they were always there—for better or for worse. What he demonstrates more than anything else is the response of an obedient, honest, and open heart, and the overruling grace and energizing power of the Holy Spirit. God placed in his hands the "keys" of the Kingdom by which the doors to the Gospel Age were opened at Pentecost, at Samaria, and finally at Caesarea. "The evening, and not the morning, was Peter's golden hour," writes Matheson. The letter which bears his name portrays a mellowed and humbled spirit, clothed by God's grace.

Another member of the inner circle was James, the son of Zebedee, a business partner with Peter and Andrew (Luke 5:10). Note how God calls and uses Christian businessmen. When Jesus asked this man and his brother John if they were able to drink of his cup of suffering, their ready answer was, "We are able." God took them at their word and gave James the honor of being the first of the apostles to suffer martyrdom for His name, almost within a decade of the time he spoke these words.

Third on the list was John, the son of Zebedee; Jesus called John and his brother James "sons of thunder." Here was a quick-tempered personality who counseled fire and sword when the gates of a Samaritan village were shut in his face. Yet in the end he becomes the apostle of love, a humbled self-effacing man; in his Gospel he called himself only "that disciple whom Jesus loved"— as a constant reminder of the love mission of the Lord Jesus.

Fourth on the list is Andrew, whose Greek name means "manly." Like Peter he was a fisherman. He used the same boat, lived in the same house, and took his place as the "finder" of his brother Peter whom he brought to Jesus. He is almost completely overshadowed by his famous brother. It was he who found the lad with the loaves and fishes. Tradition asserts his death was by crucifixion on an x-shaped cross, now called St. Andrew's cross. There is quiet and simple beauty in the characters of men such as Andrew. The Boston Sunday school teacher who paced the street in front of a shoe store and finally gathered the courage to go in and lead a young shoe salesman to Christ, is a modern Andrew who fulfilled a far greater service to the kingdom of God than he can ever know. His convert was none other than the famous evangelist D. L. Moody, whom God used to reach multitudes for the kingdom of God.

Fifth on the list is Philip, the apostle (not to be confused with Philip, the deacon). Also from "Fishersville" (Bethsaida), he may have been a boyhood friend of Andrew and Peter. Like Andrew, he is often characterized as timid and retiring. He is remembered for bringing Nathanael to Jesus (John 1:45) and for bringing Gentiles to Jesus (John 12:20-22).

Sixth on the list is Bartholomew. Again we see in this apostle a quiet and unheralded witness. Yet Armenians today honor Bartholomew, along with Thaddeus, as one who brought the gospel their way. It was the quiet, patient work of such obscure figures who contributed so much to the Church in the world of the first century. The same is true of this century.

In the apostle Matthew we have a different background. He was held in disrepute by Jews (who often classed tax collectors with harlots, not only because they relieved them of money, but because they identified them as "turncoats," collecting tribute for a foreign power). Yet in Matthew is found the very pulsebeat of Jewish patriotism, and his gospel is the "kingdom" gospel that relates as no other the coming of Jesus the Messiah to the Jewish commonwealth.

In Thomas we have the devoted apostle who preferred death to separation from His Master and who found the news of the resurrection too good to be true. His feet were among the "beautiful" feet mentioned by Paul in Romans 10 because they carried the gospel to far away India.

In James, the son of Alpheus, we have another inconspicuous figure, said to be short in stature. He is called James the "Little" or the "Less."

Simon the Zealot is the patriot who would perhaps be branded an extremist on the "far right" today. Yet the mellowing love of Christ and the cause of a Kingdom not of this world turned his gaze and his walk heavenward.

And "last of all he was seen of me also, as one born out of due time," writes the great apostle Paul who called himself the "least of the apostles." The heavenly vision he saw on the Damascus Road not only changed his personal destiny; it changed the history of the world.

This brief survey of the apostles reveals something of the kind of "clay" from which God fashioned the Church, which He inbreathed with His own Holy Spirit on the Day of Pentecost, making it a living, vital soul. Some were extroverts; most were retiring and worked in obscurity. Some were educated; most were "unlearned." Some had been politically aligned with, others against Rome. But there is one common denominator among them: all became changed men as a result of Pentecost.

The Methods of the Apostles. The New Testament and the Early Church placed little emphasis on methods as we know them today. It is a lively picture of *preaching* that is given us. If there is one apt description of the Early Church at work, it would be the concluding statement in Mark's gospel: "And they went forth, and preached every where, the Lord working with them, and confirming the word with signs following" (Mark 16:20). Yet viewed as a whole, some patterns emerge. (1) A very direct administration of the Holy Spirit in the assignment and exercise of ministries is depicted. Paul tells us, "He gave some, apostles; and some, prophets; and some, evangelists; and some, pastors and teachers; for the perfecting of the saints, for the work of the ministry, for the edifying of the body of Christ" (Ephesians 4:11, 12). There was implicit emphasis on God-called men and God-appointed ministries. (2) The mother-church concept is implied in apostolic practice. The apostles evangelized in population centers from which new converts carried the gospel message to suburbs and hinterlands in a radius extending out untold miles. It is believed Paul's work in Ephesus penetrated out for 100 miles or more and accounts for the establishment of some, if not all, of the churches mentioned in Revelation. There is reason to believe that Bible schools of one type or another developed for the training of new converts. (3) The pattern of witness was balanced between the "marketplace and the synagogue." Every church needs to have a marketplace witness outreach in addition to its "synagogue" services.

Evangelism and the Church Today. In a very real sense the ministry of the Church today is a continuation of Christ's earthly ministry. For the same reasons that Jesus said He was anointed of God, so are we: (1) To *preach* the gospel to the poor; (2) To *heal* the brokenhearted; (3) To *preach deliverance* to captives; (4) To *set at liberty* them that are bruised; and (5) To preach the *acceptable year* of the Lord. The story of the Early Church is essentially a continuation of that Jesus *began* to do and to teach (Acts 1:1). Thus the Book of Acts is never finished. Even as we examine its narrative, it is conspicuous for its unfinished character. It leaves Paul in Rome a prisoner, "preaching the kingdom of God, and teaching those things which concern the Lord Jesus Christ" (Acts 28:31). We today are called upon to pick up the story of Acts and continue it.

As a Pentecostal Movement we do well to go through this checklist of reasons why Jesus was anointed. We have known the meaning of the word "anointing," but there is a *because* that follows it. As churches, do we fulfill the purpose of our anointing? This is the real meaning of evangelism. The *why* of our Movement needs to be told in the classrooms of our Sunday schools.

8 : World Missions

It was about six o'clock one early summer evening when Jesus and His disciples came upon the rich plain of Samaria, surrounded by rolling hills. The terrain opens up to the west where the Vale of Shechem intersects it with a narrow pass, which penetrates between two mountain sentinels—Mt. Ebal on the north and Mt. Gerizim on the south. In the plain to the east as far as the eye could sweep, the fields were "already white unto harvest." The Lord led His disciples to the highway intersection at the well of Jacob.

There He rested while the disciples went into the little village of Sychar at the base of Mt. Ebal, a short distance away, to purchase food provisions. His reverie was interrupted by the sound of footsteps coming toward the well. It was a lone woman from the village, and her encounter with Jesus is beautiful.

But what is especially significant for our present study is Jesus' statement to the disciples when they returned from the village. It concerns the *harvest*. His words echo down the corridors of time, and we can still hear Him say, "The fields . . . are white already to harvest" (John 4:35). Twice Jesus used the analogy of the harvest with reference to garnering souls of men into the kingdom of God. Once it was in the setting of personal evangelism here at Jacob's well. Another time it was in the setting of what might be called "mass evangelism" when he sent out the 70 into "every city and place, whither he himself would come" (Luke 10:1, 2).

The Missionary Nature of Pentecost. Pentecost was peculiarly a harvest feast. Its background is described in Leviticus 23:15-22, and its spiritual significance derives from this background. Harvest in Palestine commences in April, about the time of the Passover feast. In fact, the Feast of Firstfruits at Passover was the high priest presenting the first sheaf of grain to the Lord. Pentecost marked the conclusion of grain harvest. There is a development in the Church Age that interestingly parallels the Jewish feast calendar from Passover to Pentecost.

There can be little doubt that we are nearing the end of this time spectrum. What the Feast of Pentecost denoted on the Jewish calendar in ancient times, so does the modern outpouring of the Holy Spirit represent in our time. It is preparatory to the final ingathering of the grain before the Lord of the harvest returns. The Pentecostal outpouring is inseparably connected with the idea of harvest, and harvest with the idea of missions.

In the Old Testament arrangements for the Feast of Pentecost, Jewish farmers were bidden "not [to] make clean riddance" of the corners in harvesting their grain fields. Some grain was to be left for the "poor and . . . the stranger" (Leviticus 23:22). Both of these terms have spiritual meaning in the New Testament. Jesus was anointed to preach the gospel to the *poor* (Luke 4:18). Throughout the Bible, men devoid of spiritual grace are often said to be poor. Even a professing church was pronounced poor by Jesus (Revelation 3:17). Poverty by Biblical standards has nothing to do with annual income but with spiritual condition. In like manner the word "stranger" has to do with persons outside the family of God (Ephesians 2:19). The gospel is intended for those without the Church.

We need to follow up on this concept. When Jesus sent out the disciples before Pentecost, He specifically told them to stay away from Gentile and Samaritan cities (Matthew 10:5, 6). But after Pentecost a radical change took place. In the words of the Great Commission it was to *all* nations that the Church was to take the gospel (Matthew 28:19).

The symbolism at the Feast of Pentecost depicted a missionary thrust. The offerings also imply this emphasis. At the Feast of Firstfruits it was the single sheaf of grain that was held before the Lord; at Pentecost it was a twin loaf of bread "baken with leaven," signifying that now both Jew and Gentile *in Christ* are *one* body. As the high priest lifted up the loaf of bread, so both Jew and Gentile are elevated to heavenly places "in Christ" (Ephesians 1:3).

There is something relevantly instructive to us in the "traditional" Pentecostal Movement. Like Peter, we may find it difficult to reconcile God manifesting His grace in pouring out the Holy Spirit upon what to us theologically may seem like "creeping things." But perhaps we should take direction from Peter and the apostles. When the Spirit fell upon these most unlikely candidates, "They held their peace and glorified God" (Acts 11:18). Holiness always follows such works of God's grace (Acts 15).

The Phenomenon of the Day of Pentecost and Missions. We have already noted that the symbols of the baptism of the Holy Spirit given by John the Baptist were symbols from the harvest process. The *wind* was the agent used to separate the chaff and other foreign debris from the grain. The *fire* was the agent that burned up these foreign elements. While they have symbolic meaning to believers, the baptism in the Spirit is, in itself, peculiarly related to a missionary purpose. The whole picture relates to the harvest of men to be garnered in through the preaching of the gospel.

Pentecost is peculiarly *missionary* in its thrust. Harry R. Boer, in *Pentecost and Missions* said, "The missionary witness of the Church begins at the precise moment of the descent of the Spirit, and the place and power of the Spirit to that witness are repeatedly attested in the book to its very end."

As the flame of fire sat upon each of the 120 at Pentecost, it suggested the manner in which this movement would spread as fire in growing conflagration. One of the remarkable characteristics about the modern Pentecostal Movement is its universality. It is not localized. Read the story of the outpouring at the turn of the century, and you will see how it did indeed spread like fire. This is no less true among the "old line" denominations today than it was in the Movement which produced the Assemblies of God. But the very fact is it is missionary in its implication, and it accords with the growth pattern of the Early Church: "They went forth, and preached every where, the Lord working with them" (Mark 16:20). When persecution hit the church in Jerusalem and "they were all scattered abroad" (Acts 8:1), it was like scattering live coals of fire throughout the land.

A Pentecostal movement is peculiarly a missionary movement. Harry Boer, in the work already cited, says, "The most rapidly developing group of churches in the world today is doubtless the grouping known as the 'Pentecostal movement.' In somewhat more than a generation it has swept beyond the boundaries of its American origins into every corner of the world. The movement is so massive that as a matter of religious and ecclesiastical significance it has been called, next to Protestantism and Roman Catholicism, Christianity's 'third force'."

In this relationship it is significant that at the very first

General Council of the Assemblies of God at Hot Springs, Arkansas, in 1914, no less than $10,000 was raised for missions from among a comparatively small group of men who filled one room. In 1969 missions giving in the Assemblies of God reached the ten-million dollar mark. And for the last 27 months to the point of this writing, each month's missions giving has been greater than that month's offering in the previous year.

Overseas adherents of the Assemblies of God, which is the product of the Movement's missionary outreach, is three times that in the United States. Our Movement's missionary force now exceeds 1,000—a figure which advances our missionary task force to fifth among all denominations in the United States.

These statistics should both instruct and challenge us. There is no room in them for pride or self-glory or for resting. The laborers are always *few* compared to the enormity of the harvest. What these statistics demonstrate is simply that now, as in the days of the apostles, the practical index or product of the outpouring of the Holy Spirit is missions. A Pentecostal church, no matter what the organizational name, will be a *missionary* church.

The Missionary Nature of the Early Church. Missions essentially is evangelism extended to the "regions beyond." Distance does not determine where a mission field begins, however. Hence the Scripture knows nothing of foreign missions in contrast to home missions. It speaks only of *world* missions, starting at the center of the home church and radiating out into circles of missionary witness unto the uttermost part of the earth. A *radiation* concept of missions is implicit in the very structure of the Book of Acts. It is implicit in the instructions of Jesus that the Apostles and the Church should be witnesses from the epic center of Jerusalem—working *outward* to the uttermost part of the earth. It was the pattern employed by

Paul at Ephesus and elsewhere. Of his work at Ephesus, the Acts record states, "So that all they which dwelt in Asia heard the word of the Lord Jesus, both Jews and Greeks" (Acts 19:10). The missions policy of the Early Church was to give the widest diffusion possible to the gospel.

The picture portrayed in the Acts record is vivid. Philip was dispatched to Samaria, then to the desert where he met the Ethiopian eunuch—thus extending the witness into Africa. Peter, with his ingrained Jewishness, is dispatched to Caesarea to introduce the gospel to the Gentiles. Antioch soon displaces Jerusalem as the Christian center from which the missionary enterprise of the Church worked out.

Portrait of a Missionary. No one exemplifies the missionary outreach of the Early Church more aptly than the apostle Paul. No one fulfilled the meaning of the word *Apostle* ("sent one") more literally and fully than Paul. As we put his life into panorama, we first see him with his traveling party halted beside the road on the edge of the green, fertile Damascan plain. It is noon. A heavenly vision of Jesus was to change the ultimate destination and purpose of that trip. Paul did go on to Damascus—but his life-direction was changed! After he recovered his sight, receiving the Holy Spirit in the same instant, his first impulse was to proclaim the deity and the Messiahship of Jesus in the Jewish synagogues of Damascus (Acts 9:20-22). Then to the Arabian desert, which spread beyond the Damascan plain like a vast land ocean, Paul journeyed alone to ponder the meaning of what happened to him and its implications for his life. This was part of his missionary preparations. He came back to Damascus after some months to face the fury of his Jewish compatriots—a fury he could understand and accept as few men could, for he himself had persecuted the Church. Then he went on to Jerusalem and ultimately to Antioch from where his missionary career was to commence.

For the second phase of Paul's apostolic career we go to the teeming metropolis of Antioch, located on the left bank of the Orontes River. To the west, some 15 miles beyond, the blue waters of the Mediterranean met the horizon. The city itself, with a first-century population approaching 500,000 persons, was set in a broad and fertile valley shielded by majestic snow-covered mountains, giving the city the name, "the Beautiful and the Golden." It became the third largest city in the Roman Empire and was the caravan center (the Chicago) of the ancient Near East. Caravans came and left the city, connecting it like a wagon wheel hub with the major travel routes to the west, north, east, and south. It was strategically located as a missions center from which to evangelize the ancient world. It was at the southern extremity of the same valley terrain, at the base of Mt. Hermon, where Jesus made His prophetic declaration, "I will build my church; and the gates of hell shall not prevail against it" (Matthew 16:18). The principle of missionary outreach from population centers, accommodating ready travel access, is seen from the outset in all the apostle's missionary enterprise.

The beginning of the first missionary journey was in a fervent prayer meeting within the city of Antioch. Jesus prescribed prayer as the first approach to missions—prayer directed to the Lord of the harvest, that He would call and send forth laborers into His harvest. Antioch is a beautiful example of obedience to this injunction. The Holy Spirit was active on the scene and expressed the mind of God on the matter, "Separate me Barnabas and Saul for the work whereunto I have called them" (Acts 13:2). The act of God calling these missionaries was followed by a demonstration of endorsement by the brethren:

"And when they had fasted and prayed, and laid their hands on them, they sent them away" (Acts 13:3).

As we follow the steps of this apostolic team from Antioch down the river to the port of Seleucia, the significance of what took place is evident in a panorama of history that comes before us. This city was a product of a political conquest by a young man from the west, Alexander the Great. Some 300 years before, he had made his "lightning conquest" of the world, and Antioch came into existence when Greek rule was established here. Now two "soldiers of the Cross" embark upon another conquest of the world—a conquest in which the church of Jesus Christ would prevail against the gates of Hades. Today that ancient city is marked by ruins and rubble and scattered peasant dwellings. But the monument left by the influence of the Apostolic Church has endured time because it was founded on eternity's foundations. Thus when Paul's ship set its bow and sailed toward the open waters of the Mediterranean and the distant island of Cyprus, there commenced a penetration of the uttermost parts of the world that has never really stopped.

Follow Paul's path from the point that his ship put in at Salamis on the east coast of Cyprus to the point where he was led out of the gates of Rome to enter the gates of glory via the stroke of an executioner's sword. Throughout we thrill to an adventure of faith and victory seldom equalled in the pages of one man's biography. It is a path that takes us from port to port, over plains, through mountain passes, and over the major imperial highways. Sometimes it was cut out of rock cliffs overhanging yawning canyons. At times it went through malaria-infested lowlands, robber-infested ravines, over high country, along winding seashores, through monument-studded desert country, and from city to city.

As we follow the path of Paul in the great cities of the ancient world, we find it would always take him first to the Jewish synagogue. Paul's guiding principle for missions was to the "Jew first, and also to the Gentile" (Romans 2:10). After he had witnessed concerning Christ in the synagogue, his path led to the marketplace (called the *agora* by the Greeks and the *forum* by the Romans). Here his message was the same. His patterns of witnessing are relevant for us today: (1) Let us not overlook Jewish evangelism in our missionary outreach. God has not given up on the Jews, neither should we (Romans 11:1). (2) There needs to be an outreach from every church into the marketplaces of our surroundings. The church's ministry is not to be confined to the synagogue (literally, the "assembly"). In the spirit of the Early Church it will reach out to the streets, the missions, jails, hospitals, rest homes, to the campus, and multitudes of other places where men and women, boys and girls are to be found.

Even more important than the geographical path Paul followed is the spiritual path he hewed out in his missionary work, Paul knew the meaning of the prayer closet. He knew the meaning of intercessory prayer (see chapter 2). He implicitly obeyed the voice and direction of the Holy Spirit—being forbidden to go to Asia on one occasion and directed by a nighttime vision to go to Macedonia. He knew what it was to have his spirit stirred within him as he looked upon the city of Athens, wholly given to idolatry. He traveled toward Corinth with urgency so that he might have opportunity to preach the gospel to the throngs that would gather nearby for the Isthmian Games. The creak of the ship's mast and sail, the orders shouted by the ship's crew, or the squealing cry of seabirds were not the things his ears heard. It was not the romance of travel but the voices of men lost without hope and without Christ that rang in his ears night and day and caused him to cry out, "I am debtor both to the Greeks, and to the Barbarians; both to the wise, and to the unwise. So, as much as in me is, I am ready to preach the gospel to you that are at Rome also. For I am not ashamed of the gospel of Christ: for it is the power of God unto salvation to every one that believeth; to the Jew first and also to the Greek" (Romans 1:14-16). He did not look upon the life of a missionary as a life of sacrifice; he declared to the church he had founded at Corinth, "For though I preach the gospel, I have nothing to glory of: for necessity is laid upon me; yea, woe is unto me, if I preach not the gospel!" (1 Corinthians 9:16).

The Missionary Growth of the Early Church. It is estimated that within the 70 years from A.D. 30 to A.D. 100, known as the apostolic period, as many as one-half million converts were won to Christ through the missionary outreach of the Early Church. Philip Schaff says that the "Pentecostal conversion of three thousand in one day at Jerusalem and the great multitude of martyrs under Nero favor a high estimate." It is believed that the converts to the Church belonged mostly to the middle and lower strata of society, and included fishermen, peasants, mechanics, traders, merchants, freedmen, and slaves.

By the time Christianity was popularized and officially recognized by the Roman Empire under Constantine in the beginning of the fourth century, it is estimated that the number may have climbed to 10 or 12 million, or about 10 percent of the population in the empire.

When we put together the indications within the Book of Acts itself, a rapid growth picture emerges, testifying to the impact of the Early Church on the world. Acts 2:41 tells of 3,000 being won to Christ on the Day of Pentecost; Acts 4:4 tells of 5,000 more soon after. Subsequent chapters use the word "multitudes" and similar references as evidence of a large ingathering of souls (Acts 5:14; 6:1, 7; 8:6, 12; 10:44, 48; 11:21, 24; 12:24, etc.).

The renowned historian on the Roman empire, Edward Gibbon, attributes the rapid spread of Christianity to five causes: (1) Christian zeal; (2) doctrine of the immortality of the soul; (3) the miracle-working power of the Early Church; (4) the standards of purity and morality of early Christians; (5) the unity and discipline of the church. But overriding all these factors is the supreme fact that it was a movement originated by God and energized by the Holy Spirit.

Missions and the Church Today. "The mission of the Church is missions," said G. Campbell Morgan. Harry Boer said, "One hardly knows where in the Book of Acts to look for a distinction between the church and missions. Tirelessly the Spirit drives the Church to witness, and continually new churches rise out of its witness. Missions was not a hobby, it was a way of life."

A truly Pentecostal church is a missionary church. The very background and meaning of Pentecost is missionary in character. From a spiritual approach (and there is really no other adequate approach), the starting point in missions is *prayer*. Missions are moved by prayer. All other aspects of the work are secondary to this one (Luke 10:2).

There are churches in our Movement with remarkable records for having sent out full-time workers from their midst. There is a high correlation between this fact and the corporate prayer life of these churches. The assembly that obeys Christ's command "pray ye," will also obey His command "go ye." If the fields were white unto harvest in Christ's day, how much more are they so today?

9 : The Supernatural

During the course of the Sunday morning service of a 2,000-member Presbyterian congregation in South America, a mother edged her way to the front of the church. In her arms was a baby, afflicted with congenital blindness; its prospect in life on this earth was dark. When the mother reached the pastor, she placed her baby in his arms and besought him to anoint and pray for a healing miracle in the baby's sightless eyes, just as she had witnessed the Pentecostals pray for the sick. Nonplussed by the unexpected development, still the pastor, perhaps more out of courtesy and sympathy for her than for any other reason, obliged her. But the unexpected happened. As the pastor prayed over the child, the miraculous healing power and virtue of the Lord Jesus Christ came into the baby's body and eyes that up to that moment were sightless, began to see. It is said that this Presbyterian congregation "went wild" with rejoicing and praise to God for what it had seen there that morning.

What the name of a congregation of believers might be makes little difference in their response when God's Spirit moves. The manifestation of the supernatural evokes faith and an expression of praise that is the same the world over. Such miracles testify to the fact that Jesus is indeed alive and is working with His church, just as He said He would do.

Again we are reminded that the story of the Early Church is essentially one of what Jesus continued to teach and to do through the agency of His church, empowered by the Holy Spirit. It is abundantly clear that teaching and doing (Acts 1:1) was intended to be achieved by the *supernatural* and under the energizing power of the Holy Spirit. It was to be the norm of the Church's experience in all times. In fact, Jesus told the apostles that they would do even greater works than He did (John 14:12) because He would go to the Father—the implication being that He would send to the Church the Holy Spirit.

What Jesus *did* vindicated what He *taught*. In the Old Testament the authentication of a prophet's message was demonstrated by a prophetic "sign." Hence Jesus challenged his unbelieving hearers to believe Him for His "works sake," if for no other reason. Now today "signs following" are still an authenticating demonstration of the gospel, convincing an unbelieving world what God's purpose and intention is for the Church. As we noted in the previous chapter, the historian Gibbon attributes this factor as one of five reasons Christianity grew so rapidly in that first century; and it is the same reason the Pentecostal Movement of the 20th century has grown so rapidly. Ironically, there are some who dispensationalize the supernatural out of the Church for now just as others scissored it out of the Bible for then. One error is as bad as the other. Dimont points to both the *human* and the *divine* witnesses to Christ—the latter being through miracles; the first through the preaching of Christ to the world. The God-intended pattern is beautifully expressed in the verse we have quoted so often, ". . . And they went forth, and preached every where, the Lord working with them, and confirming the word with signs following" (Mark 16:20).

The Intention of Christ for the Church. It needs to be kept in mind that the apostles were first called disciples, or students—then apostles. In Christ's instruction to them we have His instruction to the Church throughout the Church Age. The record states, "And when he had called unto him his twelve disciples, he gave them power against unclean spirits, to cast them out, and to heal all manner of sickness and all manner of diseases" (Matthew 10:1). The first step for ministry was the empowering act coming from Jesus Himself, who is also the Baptizer with the Holy Spirit.

The second step in his sending out the disciples was *instruction* as to what they were to do upon being sent out. It is here that we find outlined the fountainhead of the Church's ministry. It was the same ministry pattern that Jesus Himself fulfilled, and it was the ministry pattern of the Book of Acts. Let us note the outline: (1) preach, (2) heal, (3) cleanse the lepers, (4) raise the dead, and (5) cast out devils (Matthew 10:7,8).

The overriding principle of ministry is to *give out* with the same liberality with which Christ has endowed the Church. It is to be a living spring of water (see John 7:38). The implication is that some have less to give because they have not availed themselves of the resources of the Spirit. The important point is that without supernatural endowment the Church can not fulfill this ministry check list. It is a ministry to the whole man—for body, soul, and spirit. And it is a ministry that attests supernaturally to the veracity of the gospel of Christ.

It was the ministry pattern of Jesus. "And Jesus went about all Galilee, teaching in their synagogues, and preaching the gospel of the kingdom, and healing all manner of sickness and all manner of disease among the people" (Matthew 4:23). In the same context it is said, "He was moved with compassion on them." Men who minister in Christ's name and power should also minister with His compassion. Writing of Smith Wigglesworth, pioneer Pentecostal evangelist of this century, Stanley Frodsham said, "Being moved with compassion, was Smith Wigglesworth's daily experience. Tears would run copiously down his cheeks as he ministered to the afflicted. How tender he could be in dealing with children and aged folks! How he would valiantly storm heaven with his praying for the pain-racked and suffering ones."

Today Jesus continues to minister through His body—the Church. The Church is to manifest both His power and His compassion. No fact more clearly prescribes the place of the supernatural and the motivation to seek for the supernatural in the work of the Church today. The measure of the Church's compassion will parallel its supernatural power for ministry.

The Early Church and the Supernatural. The supernatural character of the Early Church issues from the very manner in which it was brought into being on the Day of Pentecost. Three words, signs, wonders, and powers, best describe the supernatural in the Book of Acts. Each points to a distinct aspect of the same operation. Power denotes the *source* of the miracle; it is the same Greek work *(dunamis)* used of the baptism of the Holy Spirit, "But ye shall receive power [*dunamis*] after that the Holy Ghost is come upon you" (Acts 1:8). *Sign* denotes the manifestation of the supernatural and the *wonder* or effect it produces upon those who witness it. These are demonstrated repeatedly in the ministry of the Early Church.

Peter, a Channel of the Supernatural. The simple faith and trust of this Galilean fisherman, Simon, was demonstrated from the start when a Stranger walked on the beach where he and his business partners were mending their nets. There was no hesitation. The record simply states, "They forsook all, and followed him" (Luke 5:11). This quality of faith in Peter was to make him a special instrument of supernatural power. His immediate and intuitive recognition of the character of Jesus and his obedience to that insight mark him as a spiritually sensitive man. This characteristic is revealed again and again. At the revelation of Christ's Messiahship near the Mount of Transfiguration, it was Peter to whom the Holy Spirit revealed the cardinal fact that the Church is forever founded upon the Lord Jesus. At the gate Beautiful in the Temple, it was Peter's sensitivity to the Spirit's voice and his unfaltering obedience to that voice that made possible a healing miracle for the lame man—and in the salvation of 5,000 other men. Such a response to some may seem to border on incredulity, but God honors and uses such men in a ministry of the supernatural.

John Wesley was said to be a person of this kind; he never questioned the manifestation of the supernatural, even though he did not understand it. At three o'clock in the morning in a London prayer meeting, the power of God descended mightily upon the 60 persons gathered there. Many fell to the floor while others cried out for joy. Then in an instant the entire company broke out with one voice, "We praise thee, O God. We acknowledge Thee to be the Lord." It was common for Wesley's hearers to fall to the ground or to cry out under conviction of sin. "Quench not the Spirit," was to Wesley a solemn warning which he scrupulously and conscientiously tried to follow. There is a quality of faith to which the Holy Spirit responds in supernatural ministry. Peter possessed such a faith. He possessed a sensitivity to the voice of the Spirit that sometimes went against his natural inclinations. Through the gift of knowledge he exposed the sin of Ananias and Sapphira within the Church, (Acts 5:3). At Samaria, it was Peter's hands laid upon believers that resulted in the outpouring of the Holy Spirit upon them (Acts 8:17). The use of *hands* in connection with the ministry of the supernatural is indeed an interesting part of the record: "And by the hands of the apostles were many signs and wonders wrought among the people; (. . . and believers were the more added to the Lord, multitudes both of men and women;) insomuch that they brought forth the sick into the streets, and laid them on beds and couches that at the least the shadow of Peter passing by might overshadow some of them . . . and they were healed every one" (Acts 5:12-16). There was an act of faith through the use of their hands, invoking the miracle-working power of God. A supernatural ministry through Peter was exercised wherever he went. In the same country where he ministered to Cornelius he was instrumental in the healing of Aenaeas of the palsy and in raising Dorcas from the dead (Acts 9:32-43). Were one to go through the Biblical record and remove from Peter's life and ministry all narratives which have to do with miracles, there would be very little left.

Peter disappears from the Biblical record as suddenly and with the same simplicity with which he appeared. The final statement concerning him is, "And he departed, and went into another place" (Acts 12:17). From this point in the Book of Acts the ministry of the apostle Paul and the missionary expansion of the Church take over.

The miracles which attest to Paul's ministry are strikingly parallel in kind and number to those wrought through Peter. God honors faith and obedience in the lives of such men. Peter, the apostle to the Jews, and Paul, the apostle to the Gentiles, exercised supernatural ministries, the comparison of which deserves study. Both were instrumental in notable healings of crippled men, lame from birth in each case. Both healings excited the wonder and awe of the crowds who witnessed it. In both instances Paul and Peter disclaimed any personal power by which the healings took place. Both men raised the dead. Both were instrumental in ministry which was attested by the outpouring of the Holy Spirit with the phenomenon of speaking in tongues. Both administered rebuke, attested by a supernatural act of judgment from God. Both were instrumental in healings by secondary agents. Even Peter's shadow falling over the sick wrought healing. In like manner, handkerchiefs or aprons from Paul's body brought healing and deliverance to the sick (Acts 19:12). Both were supernaturally delivered from prison. Both received calls to minister in new missions fields through supernatural visions or summons. Peter was prepared by a vision for the summons of the men from Cornelius' house (Acts 10), while Paul received his summons from the man appearing in his vision in the nighttime.

The point of this comparative summary is to show how God in supernatural power backed up the *witness* of the apostles in a special way. The ministries of the other apostles were attended by the supernatural as well: "And by the hands of the apostles were many signs and wonders wrought among the people" (Acts 5:12). Added to these words is this significant statement: " . . . And they were healed every one" (Acts 5:16).

Nor was the ministry of the supernatural confined to the apostles. The ministry of Philip, a deacon, was no less supernaturally attested: " . . . The people . . . gave heed unto those things which Philip spake, hearing and seeing the miracles which he did" (Acts 8:6).

Nor is the ministry of the supernatural confined in the Book of Acts to miraculous *deeds*. There were miracles of utterance. The gift of the Holy Spirit on the Day of

Pentecost was attested by the miraculous utterance in other tongues. The utterance of prophecy was so prominent in the Early Church that certain individuals were distinguished for the exercise of a prophetic ministry; included in this group were Barnabas, Simeon, Lucius, and Manaen (foster brother of Herod). The four daughters of Philip, the evangelist, are examples of the fulfillment of Joel's prophecy that God would pour out the Spirit and give the prophetic gift to young women as well as young men.

Not only did the supernatural power of the Spirit operate in the realm of the physical and in utterance, but it also operated in the realm of the intellectual. It endowed the apostles and the Early Church with knowledge and insight. "For to one is given by the Spirit the word of wisdom; to another the word of knowledge by the same Spirit" (1 Corinthians 12:8). The Bible says Stephen's opponents "were not able to resist the wisdom and the spirit by which he spake" (Acts 6:10). Paul spoke under an anointing of the Spirit's power and wisdom that defied and confounded the wise of this world (1 Corinthians 1:27; 2:7). James described the behavioral patterns that stem from God-given wisdom in contrast with worldly wisdom. There is a supernatural dimension to wisdom and to the realm of the intellect that few know. The Spirit of God is omniscient as well as omnipresent and omnipotent. God's family is invited to draw upon His intelligence as well as upon His power. It is clearly the intent of the Holy Spirit to endue the Church and believers with power that supernaturally energizes the whole person—spirit, body, and intellect.

Take the miracles out of the Book of Acts and there is little left. The fact remains that God made abundant use of them in giving the Church a start, and there is not the slightest hint that He ever intended to "phase them out" of the Church's ministry.

The Supernatural and the Church Today. It is significant that the emphasis within the ranks of the modern Pentecostal Movement on the baptism in the Holy Spirit has brought with it a ministry of supernatural power of the same character experienced by the apostles and the Early Church. Harry Boer in his *Pentecost and Missions* says of the Pentecostals that "their emphases are on simple preaching of the gospel, prayer, the gift of the Spirit, accompanied by speaking with tongues, faith healing, and prophecy." The same description would have to be made of the Apostolic Church.

The outpouring of the Spirit at the turn of the century was a spontaneous movement at many places, and in every instance it was accompanied by supernatural signs and wonders which corresponded in kind and character with those in the Book of Acts. As one reads accounts of these early visitations of the Spirit, he is impressed with one fact: The signs in themselves were not the object of quest in those days. Frank Bartleman, in describing a typical meeting at the Azusa Street Mission in Los Angeles, wrote of the ministry of a Holiness preacher, W. J. Seymour. "Brother Seymour generally sat behind two empty show boxes, one on top of the other. He usually kept his head inside the top one during the meeting in prayer. There was no pride there. The service ran almost continuously. Seeking souls could be found under the power almost any hour, day or night. People came to meet God. He was always there, hence the continuous meeting. God's presence became more and more wonderful. In that old building, with its low rafters and bare floor, God took strong men and women to pieces, and put them together again for His glory. It was a tremendous overhauling process. Pride, self-assertion, self-importance, and self-esteem could not survive there. No one knew what might be coming, what God would do. All was spontaneous, all of the Spirit. We wanted to hear from God through whomsoever He might speak. We had no respect of persons"

A Baptist minister describing one of the services there said, "As Brother Seymour preached, God's power seemed increasing in him. Near the close of the sermon, as suddenly as on the day of Pentecost, while I was sitting in front of the preacher, the Holy Spirit fell upon me and literally filled me. . . . I had not been seeking the gift of tongues or any gift; but oh, how I did long for God Himself to completely fill me, and in His great love he surely did!" This same man went to Egypt and was used in a mighty ministry of intercession that produced great spiritual results, notably the Lillian Trasher Orphanage at Assiut.

The Spirit of God moved convincingly and dynamically on a broad front of human needs not only in Los Angeles but in other places where the Pentecostal outpouring came. In 1906, one paper, the *Apostolic Faith,* reported, "Hundreds of souls have received salvation and healing. The Lord God is in Los Angeles in different missions and churches in mighty power in spite of opposition."

It would be a practical and worthwhile thing for every Sunday school worker, youth leader, and church officer in our churches to read or reread prayerfully Stanley Frodsham's *With Signs Following,* an account of the outpouring of the Spirit in this 20th century that produced our Assemblies of God movement among others.

God is not through visiting His people in supernatural power. There is every evidence that He is penetrating churches traditionally quite diverse from the so-called "Pentecostal" churches. The "charismatic movement," as it is called, points to an exciting uplook at a time when the outlook is not optimistic. The steeple of a large brick church edifice in the university district of one of our large west coast cities points upward with hope in a new context. For within its walls has come the sound of a mighty rushing wind from heaven—filling believers with the Holy Spirit in tarrying meetings, never before associated with such an institution. While there are some decided differences of theological viewpoint, traditions, and practices, the significant fact is that God is moving by His Spirit in supernatural power and demonstration.

The Supernatural and the Future. The Bible indicates that as time draws to an end, the world will witness an accelerated spiritual contest in the realm of the supernatural. Satan is going to presume to work miracles in the same manner as did the magicians of Egypt when God called forth His people from that land with a mighty demonstration of His supernatural power. History will repeat itself as the world prepares for the greatest exodus that it has ever seen—this one too by the supernatural power of God when Jesus comes for His church. Satan will contest God's move, as did Pharoah the exodus of Israel. One of the striking statements concerning the end-time by John the Revelator is this: "And I saw three unclean spirits like frogs come out of the mouth of the dragon, and out of the mouth of the beast, and out of the mouth of the false prophet. For they are the spirits of devils, working miracles, which go forth unto the kings of the earth and of the whole world, to gather them to the battle of that great day of God Almighty" (Revelation 16: 13, 14). Political leaders will be "magnetized."

The full bloom of this spirit will burst forth in the presence of the Man of Sin when he is revealed in the end of time. In the meantime the spiritual winds are making themselves felt with increasing velocity, and the Church must reckon with this factor. The frustrations of the Church are legion. A new generation is fast arising which "knows not the Lord," and this fact is grooming an atmosphere in which spiritual deception will find fertile ground. The present-day move toward occultism and the forbidden denotes another spiritual wind of demonic origins. The best defense is a strong offense. The resources that enabled the Apostolic Church have not been withdrawn. Our task is a spiritual one, requiring spiritual equipment: "Finally, my brethren, be strong in the Lord, and in the power of his might" (Ephesians 6:10).

10 : The Second Coming

Flying high over the Mediterranean Sea, we were treated to one of the most spectacular sights to be found in the Mediterranean world. Across the great peninsula known today as Turkey, the snow-capped Pontus mountains towered up at the far northern perimeter bordering the Black Sea. The southern perimeter was ringed by the famous Taurus mountains, bordering the Mediterranean. This mountain wall was penetrated numerous times by the apostles, especially Paul, in order to carry the gospel to this region.

Below us the Island of Rhodes, one of the important ancient seaports, came into sharp outline. Here the shipping lanes of the ancient world converged in the days of wind-powered sea travel. Then the island-studded coast of ancient Asia began to emerge as the huge jet winged its way toward Athens. As it began to descend for the landing, the rugged coastline of the Greek Peninsula came into view, with Mt. Olympus rearing its domed peak in the distance.

Within the sweep of this view the letters from three apostles were sent to various destinations, places which had been touched by their labors in the gospel. All dominantly relate to the second coming of Christ. They came from the apostles John, Peter, and Paul.

Christ's Return, the Vital Expectation of the Early Church. The question of the apostles just before Christ's ascension, "Wilt thou restore Israel at this time?" was not an irrelevant one. Nor was Jesus' answer irrelevant to the question. He told them to tarry for the coming of the Holy Spirit in Jerusalem. R. A. Nelson points out, "Everywhere in the New Testament, the Holy Spirit is spoken of in eschatological ("end-time") terms. . . . The striking phenomenon of Pentecost itself . . . is the preaching of the gospel to all nations." These were in themselves *end-time* signs.

The Jewish rabbis of that time taught that the Messiah would appear in the end time when Israel's plight as a nation would be in desperate straits. They held there would be signs to announce Messiah's coming: restlessness, war, pestilence, famine, drought, crop failure, and a turning away from God. They also held that the coming of the Messiah would mark the end of the present age. Israel would be restored; and after Messiah rules for a period, an age of unending bliss will begin. All this was taught by the *rabbis*. All this adds meaning to the apostles' question, "Wilt thou restore Israel at this time?" The answer came at Pentecost. It was revealed to Peter that they had, in fact, entered into the "last days." The outpouring of the Spirit and the witness of the Church was, in fact, an evidence that the time of Joel's prophecy had commenced. In a Biblical sense the entirety of the Church Age, from Pentecost until Christ's return, comes within the scope of the "last days." Pentecost, by its very definition, and purpose, is very much related to the second coming of Jesus.

It is significant that in the modern Pentecostal Movement there came frequent and repeated utterance by the Spirit on the subject of the second coming of Christ. The pulse-beat emphasis of Pentecost is not only witness and missions but the imminency of the second coming of Jesus.

The Book of Acts and the Second Coming. We normally do not think of the Book of Acts for its bearing on the second coming of Christ. Yet the message is there. It is prominently featured in the preaching of the apostles. In the first two sermons by Peter the Second Coming is regarded as imminent, and *repentance* and baptism is the only way of salvation. Peter's quotation from David, "Until I make thy foes thy footstool" (Acts 2:35), referred to Christ's coming in vengeance the second time. It lent urgency to the need for the nation to repent. The thrust of their messages was that God is granting the world one more opportunity. This was the "good tidings" of apostolic preaching. Even though the Jews had incurred to themselves God's severest penalty by crucyifying Jesus (Acts 3:14), yet another opportunity was offered by which all men may escape "the wrath to come." Paul used the word "vengeance" in the ancient concept of blood vengeance. When a kinsman suffered death at the hands of another, the next of kin deemed it their duty to execute vengeance upon the perpetrators of the crime. This principle is still to be seen on an international scale between Arabs and Jews today. In the death of Jesus, rejectors of His grace come under the sentence of death, calling for blood vengeance. This is why the apostles, especially Peter, called upon Israel to repent and be baptized.

The same message Peter preached to the nation of Israel, Paul preached to the *Gentiles*. In Paul's Mars' Hill address he points to the same theme: "Because he hath appointed a day, in the which he will judge the world in righteousness by that man whom he hath ordained" (Acts 17:31). It is noteworthy that the imperative direction given to the world at every mention of Christ's *second coming* is repent. It was the same message preached by John the Baptist at Christ's *first coming.* Those churches which today take seriously the message of the second coming of Christ are also the ones that preach *repentance*. Moreover, the fervent witness and missionary outreach of the apostles and the Early Church cannot be separated from a vital expectation of Christ's imminent return. The whole thrust of the apostles' lives, their value system in life, were shaped by the vital expectation that "this same Jesus, which is taken up from you into heaven, shall so come in like manner as ye have seen him go into heaven" (Acts 1:11). We see this illustrated in the life of the Church time and again. They left settled vocations to carry the gospel. They endured persecution of the worst sort to be witnesses unto Christ. Some sold their possessions and placed the money in a common treasury, so certain were they of Christ's soon return.

The Second Coming and What the Apostles Taught Concerning Everyday Life. In the apostolic preaching in Acts we have seen what the apostles said to the *outside world* concerning Christ's second coming. It was "repent." We now turn attention to what they had to say to the Church on the subject. We draw upon three examples among the apostles: John, Peter, and Paul.

John and the Future. Among the apostles, the two sons of Zebedee fulfill distinct roles of suffering for the Name and sake of Jesus. Their careers in this respect commence from that moment when they answered Jesus, "We are able," when He asked them if the ambitions they expressed to *reign* with Him could be matched by willingness and ability to *suffer* with Him. We have already discussed the early martyrdom of James. We now turn attention to the other brother who, according to tradition, nearly suffered martyrdom in a boiling cauldron of oil but was miraculously delivered.

It was A.D. 95, the 14th year of Emperor Domitian's reign in Rome. The scene was a barren island of red and gray volcanic rocks which formed quaint formations along its seacoast. This dreary setting is about 30 miles off the coast of Asia Minor (Turkey). According to the ancient church historians and writers, Irenaeas, Eusebius, Jerome, and others, the apostle John was exiled that year as part of a Roman *purge* against the Christian *sect*—regarded as a threat to the Roman way of life.

About a half-mile up the hill from the one town on this 22-square-mile island, said to be in the shape of a horse's head, is a cave where John is supposed to have received his visions. The spot is not so important as what he saw. The curtains were drawn aside from a gigantic stage whereon the great drama of the future was enacted before his eyes. Writing with imagination and with some knowledge of the setting of this scene, Henry M. Field said, "Again, he (John) stood upon the cliff, his white hair streaming in the wind, and now the clouds rolling upon the horizon, the flashes of lightning from which lighted up at once the dark heavens above and the angry sea below . . . these were images . . . of judgments that were coming on the earth. And when he speaks of one 'whose voice was as the sound of many waters' the very expression is an echo of the deep."

The book which this apostle wrote at the instruction of Jesus is called the Book of Revelation, or more literally, the "unveiling of Jesus Christ." The message of the second coming of Christ in majesty and glory is at the center and circumference of the book. The very first episode John saw is expressed in his opening words, "Behold, he cometh with clouds; and every eye shall see him, and they also which pierced him: and all kindreds of the earth shall wail because of him. Even so, Amen" (Revelation 1:7). The book concludes with the same message in the form of a declaration and a prayer: "He which testifieth these things saith, Surely I come quickly. Amen. Even so, come, Lord Jesus" (Revelation 22:20). The coming of Christ in judgment upon the world, of which the apostles spoke so often in the Book of Acts, is depicted here as it will be in prophetic fulfillment. But we are especially interested in the practical instruction that Christ, through the apostle, gives to the Church. Even as the declarations on the Second Coming have been drawn from the first and last passages of the book, so are the accompanying *instructions* to the Church. The practical thrust for the Church of then and today is to be found in Christ's messages to the seven churches, actual churches located in the Roman province of Asia within a hundred-mile radius of Ephesus; Ephesus was the center of evangelism from which the apostles ministered (tradition holds that here John lived out his days after the Patmos vision). Christ is presented as judge over the Church and the world. His message to the Church is most easily singled out by the imperatives He used: "Remember . . . repent . . . do first works . . . fear none of . . . things thou shalt suffer . . . repent . . . be watchful . . . strengthen things which remain . . . remember, hold fast, and repent . . . hold fast . . . buy of me gold tried in the fire . . . white raiment, anoint thine eyes." We have selected these instructions of Christ because they were also the concerns of the Apostolic Church. The one word recurring most often is *repent*. In the context of the Second Coming theme it is the same word which recurrs in the messages of the apostles to the world. It is a word that is relevant and instructive to us today. In time of need, a repenting church finds strength and resources from Christ. It is a word that implies sensitivity to sin and impurity of life. It is specifically the work of the Holy Spirit to convict of sin, of righteousness, and of judgment to come. In the light of Christ's coming, O, may we as a people dedicated to the emphasis upon the Holy Spirit ask Him to sensitize our hearts to sin. Here is one of the most practical preparations for His *parousia* (coming again).

The last part of John's vision moves with the same burden and concern for the Church: "He that is unjust, let him be unjust still; and he which is filthy, let him be filthy still: and he that is righteous, let him be righteous still; and he that is holy, let him be holy still. And, behold, I come quickly; and my reward is with me, to give every man according as his work shall be" (Revelation 22: 11, 12). As the indictments of Christ against the seven churches are studied, they are seen to revolve largely around the concerns of the first church council recorded in Acts 15: the heresies of "fornication" and "eating of things sacrificed to idols." Because sexual vice was a part of heathen worship, the sensual allurements of Diana worship at Ephesus and other cities in the apostolic circuit had a tremendous appeal to the baser elements of human nature. Today the same thing has made inroads into some elements of the professing church under the rationalization of the "new morality." The message of the Second Coming carries with it a corollary message of holiness and purity. This is the message from Christ through John.

Peter and the Future. From the pen of Peter comes some hint of his missionary work through the two letters which bear his name. He addressed himself to the "strangers scattered throughout Pontus, Galatia, Cappadocia, Asia and Bithynia" (1 Peter 1:1). These were names of places bordering the Black Sea on the northern perimeter of what is now Turkey. The coastline is a rugged one with mountains rising abruptly from the sea to heights of six to seven thousand feet. Throughout this region were small groups of Christians; these people worked in the timber industry, in shipbuilding, in mining, or in agriculture. An ill wind was blowing from Rome. Christians since the burning of Rome by Nero were kept under a suspicious eye and were considered a threat to the well-being of the empire. Hence Peter's first letter was to prepare Christians for the "fiery trials" about to try their faith (1 Peter 1:7).

Peter's second epistle was his farewell letter, just as 2 Timothy was Paul's farewell letter. Both apostles faced the immediate prospects of execution for "crimes against the state." Just as Paul points a warning finger to an apostacizing *laity* in the last days, Peter does so toward an apostacizing *clergy*. In order to understand what is taking place in the Church today, these two letters deserve careful and repeated study. Nothing analyzes current trends so accurately as these two letters of prophetic description.

The thrust of Peter's words are both positive and negative. He enjoins Christians to submit to their pastoral leadership—he refers to the pastors as shepherds. It was for the "younger to submit to the elder" and for all to be subject one to another in humility (1 Peter 5:1-5). The thrust of this instruction is identical to that which Jesus gave to the disciples when He spoke about His return (Matthew 24:38-51). A spirit of submission and love runs counter to the prevailing spirit of rebellion in the world (Matthew 24:12) and the coldness of love which goes along with it.

The second insight Peter gave the Early Church concerns what he calls "false teachers" in the Church. Peter characterized them in a twofold manner: (1) Scoffers. This word denotes an intellectual attitude; and (2) sensual: "Walking after their own lusts." This word denotes their moral attitude. It is significant that these two qualities very frequently go together. The proponents of the new morality within the Church are hardly persons who believe in the imminent return of Jesus Christ. They scoff at the idea of the supernatural and pass it off as a "primitive vestige of a superstitious and unscientifically enlightened age."

Moreover, Peter tells us that these teachers argue on a "uniformitorian" basis, that is, "all things remain the same as they always have." Divine intervention in world affairs, sometimes call *catastrophism,* is to them unscientific. But Peter tells us God's prophetic calendar moves surely toward a cataclysmic and universal day of judgment. Peter called attention to the Flood in the time of Noah and said it would be repeated, but with fire. Whatever might be the outcome archaeologically, it seems interesting that in our day the world's attention is focused on the search for the remains of Noah's Ark on Mt. Ararat. Perhaps the very search is God's way of calling the world's attention to coming judgment and to Christ's second coming. The burden of Peter's message is hope.

Paul and the Future. We move now to the third apostle who gave the Early Church and us some of the grandest insights on the second coming of Jesus, especially concerning the conditions that would precede His coming. Let us join the apostle as he followed the famous Via Egnatia along the Aegean sea coast from Philippi to Thessalonica. Hemmed between the mountains to the west and the sea to the east, the road ascended the foothills of the Cortiates Mountains; then it dropped down into Thessalonica, which arched around the largest gulf on the Balkan Peninsula like a great amphitheater. A forest of ships' masts in the harbor would have marked the city, with its population of 200,000 in Paul's day, as a naval base and a shipping center. To the west, Mt. Olympus rears in clear view to a height of over nine thousand feet. Its glittering snow-covered dome was held by ancients to be the throne of Zeus, who held council with the gods of Greece there.

It was here in the city of Thessalonica that the apostle Paul was used of God in planting the gospel seed which grew into a great church. Paul had both a revival and a riot here; and in the interests of personal safety, he was obliged to leave. But Paul never forgot this church. They took the message of Christ's coming with such seriousness that they sold their property to await His return. Their error is less serious than that of a worldly, indulgent, sleepy, and unalert church. It was the latter extreme that evoked Christ's most severe rebuke, and that dishonors His name more than the mistakes of the Thessalonian church. Nevertheless the error of Thessalonica called forth from Paul some of the grandest insights concerning the Second Coming. Especially this is so with reference to the world religious conditions as they will be before Jesus returns to earth. The phenomenon of Jesus returning in the air with a shout and with the voice of the archangels and with the trump of God signals the resurrection of the dead in Christ (1 Thessalonians 4:16, 17); the event constitutes a bequest of comfort that the Church of all ages has drawn upon: "Comfort one another with these words" (1 Thessalonians 4:18).

Paul's second letter to this church puts the question of the *time* of Christ's return in correct perspective. The apostle skillfully deals with the *problem* of delay in Christ's return, pointing to three trends which will signal that return: (1) the "falling away" within the Church (Greek: *apostasia,* from whence we get our word apostasy); (2) the revealing of the Man of Sin; and (3) the taking away of the restraining force against iniquity in the world. (These trends are, without question, in process at this present moment.) It is such teaching that provides the touchstone of alertness, of which Jesus spoke in His Olivet discourse. After outlining the signs of His second coming, Jesus gave the disciples three practical instructions for these days: *Watch, take heed,* (mental and physical conditioning for such times), and *pray.* These three characteristics of living go together. A praying people will be a watchful people and a self-disciplined people. An indulgent, affluent, and yet worried western society is finding itself unable to cope mentally with world conditions as they exist today. The prophetic Scriptures, including this one, call for as prayerful and careful study today as when they were first given to the Early Church by the apostles. In short, Paul's prescription for the Thessalonian problem was the same as that given by Jesus: "Occupy until I come." The task of witnessing, if anything, should be intensified before the end comes.

There is yet a final scene concerning Paul and the future. It is in a *prison in Rome,* where the great apostle awaits the executioner's sword. If it was the Mamertime Prison at the edge of Capitoline Hill just north of the forum, it was a dark, damp, dingy, rock-hewn cavern with no opening except in the ceiling through which the prisoners were thrown and food was dropped. From here the apostle wrote his farewell letter to Timothy and us. He describes in detail the "last days," describing them as "perilous times." Then he details them with a list of some 20 characteristics. The persons he describes are to be found within the professing church, and his counsel is "from such turn away" (2 Timothy 3:5).

What are the resources for times like these? Let each of the apostles tell us in a word. From John's writings, it is the Holy Spirit. "But ye have an unction from the Holy One, and ye know all things" (1 John 2:20). From Paul's, it is God's Word: "But continue thou in the things which thou hast learned . . . that from a child thou hast known the holy scriptures, which are able to make thee wise unto salvation through faith" (2 Timothy 3:14). (This is where the Sunday school comes into the picture.) From Peter, it is "grow in grace, and in the knowledge of our Lord and Saviour Jesus Christ" (2 Peter 3:18). *Grace* calls for dependence on the merit, the strength, and the power of Christ. It is an attitude. Knowledge of Jesus points to knowing Him experientially as the Holy Spirit and His Word reveal Him. For every problem situation, the apostles have pointed to a resource.

The Blessed Hope and the Church Today. A living and dynamic hope of Christ's return was part and parcel of apostolic living and thinking. It has been one of the special emphases of our own Pentecostal Movement. It is true that some have made mistakes in identifications on particulars, yet it is to their credit that they have been possessed of a spirit of watchfulness. We, as a Spirit-filled people, need to take care that we not become neutralized or fearful of studying, preaching, and teaching the prophetic themes from the Bible "for fear of controversy," or because some may have made mistakes in the past. Certainly no more than we would abandon our other Pentecostal beliefs because some have erred concerning them.

If the Apostolic Church lived in the *beginning* of the "last days," how much closer do we live to their conclusion. Let our total outlook center in the final words of the Bible: "Surely I come quickly," and our prayer, "Even so, come Lord Jesus" (Revelation 22:20).